ARISTOTLE'S POETICS

TRANSLATION AND ANALYSIS

Aristotle's Poetics
Translation and Analysis

By

Kenneth A. Telford

Gateway Editions, Ltd.

South Bend, Indiana

To My Wife

Nancy Jo

Copyright © 1961 by Kenneth A. Telford

Published by Gateway Editions, Limited
  120 West LaSalle Street, South Bend, Indiana 46601

Manufactured in the United States of America, 6–78

Library of Congress Catalog Card Number: 60-53611

International Standard Book Number: 0-89526-932-5

CONTENTS

ARISTOTLE'S POETICS: ANALYSIS

PREFACE

Man's artistic works are a persistent fact throughout his recorded history, and the energy and talent which he has devoted to art have rivaled those displayed in any field. But as in those other fields, man is seldom satisfied with the fact alone. He must ask the question "Why?" In the case of art the result has been a great volume of writings which nowadays we refer to as aesthetics. Some of these inquiries into the nature of art have been worked out in great detail, while others have been but briefly sketched or simply implied in the context of other problems. The value of these writings, too, has varied a great deal. Some have contributed little to our appreciation of art, but there are many that have immensely enriched our understanding and enjoyment by giving us insights into aesthetic values that might otherwise have escaped us. Indeed, from the standpoint of the audience, it is this function of enlarging our capacity to apprehend the meanings embodied in art works, and therefore of enlivening our response to those works, that gives aesthetic inquiry its ultimate justification. For great art is seldom transparent to the untutored. Most of us need guidance in sharpening our sensibilities to what art offers us.

Of all those who have turned to the investigation of aesthetic problems, probably none has enjoyed an influence on subsequent thought comparable to that of Aristotle. Even those who dispute what he had to say about art commonly acknowledge his importance by constructing their theories in opposition to his or what they suppose to be his. Many of the terms and dis-

tinctions used in the discussion of art are derived from
his writings, though they may be given quite different
meanings and used for quite different purposes. Moreover, in recent years, especially in the English-speaking
world, there has been a renewed interest in the formu-
lation of aesthetic inquiry more or less along the lines
which he set forth.

In this translation of the *Poetics* the primary concern
has been to make as literal a reproduction of Aristotle's
words as is consistent with readability. I have not tried
to give the treatise any grace or facility of expression
which the Greek text lacks. Nor have I tried to make
the translation an interpretive reconstruction of what
might be presumed to be Aristotle's intention. Interpretations and interpolations which go beyond what
the text will literally support not only suffer from the
fact that the translator may err in his interpretation of
the text's meaning, but they also preclude the possibility of the reader's deciding for himself the adequacy
of the interpretation. Therefore, where additional expressions were deemed necessary for the establishment
of sense they have been marked off from the literal
translation by brackets or relegated to footnotes.

To the fullest extent possible, consistent with intelli-
gibility, a single Greek word has been rendered by a
single English word. Many translators feel that this
practice is suspect on the assumption that the Greek
word shifts its meaning in different contexts. This assumption, I am convinced, is inimical to Aristotle's
philosophic method. But even if it were true that Aristotle uses words analogically as Plato does, and not
univocally, the shift in meaning would have to be fixed
by the context and not by the word itself, and there
would still have to be a reason why he uses the same
Greek word. In fairness to the reader who cannot read
Greek the identity of the word must be made evident
so that he may judge for himself, not only the reason
why the word is repeated, but even whether or not the

word is analogical. Still there are passages in which, because of the nature of the languages involved, this ideal cannot be adhered to, for both languages have words with a breadth of function to which no word in the other language can do justice. Therefore, if more than one Greek word has been translated by a single English word they are separately listed in the index under the English word, and if more than one English word has been used to translate a given Greek word the variants are listed after the Greek word in the index. The Greek word has been included in the index to allow the reader, if he chooses, to make use of a Greek lexicon. As a result of adhering to these principles the translation will, I think, allow a much closer reading of the *Poetics* in English than has heretofore been possible. Especially important in this regard is the translation of connectives without which the articulation of the argument is lost.

But even if it be granted that a translation of a philosophic work should avoid excesses of interpretation, still the writings of Aristotle that have come down to us are of such a nature that a person picking up his work for the first time cannot proceed very far without feeling an urgent need for guidance. For Aristotle's extant writings are notoriously crabbed, and the coherence of his argument is difficult to penetrate. And yet ancient writers who had access to writings of his that have disappeared with the ages attest his command of language and the lucidity and sublimity of his style. He was, in fact, reputed to have been a very fine poet. It has been suggested by scholars that those writings of his which have come down to us are either notes from which he lectured to his students at the Lyceum, or private records of his observations and investigations, or even simply notes taken by his students from his lectures. In any case, there can be no doubt that they are not his published works.

Therefore, an analysis of the argument of the *Poetics*

has been added to the translation to help the reader in
following the thread of Aristotle's discussion. An analysis of a text has three related aspects to its goal of making the text comprehensible. It should develop the meanings of the key terms employed, clarify the procedure
by which the problem of the treatise is attacked, and
make evident the considerations which ground or vali-
date the argument as a whole. The analysis is an attempt
to handle all three aspects in such a way as to exhibit
the unity of the treatise. To accomplish this the analysis
searches for the main divisions into which the argument
naturally falls, establishes the problem which each division faces, and then subdivides these divisions so as
to articulate the subordinate problems. It has therefore
been possible to divide the analysis into sections corresponding to the main divisions of the text itself. The
analytical table of contents which precedes the translation will give the reader an outline of the various divisions of the *Poetics* as they are discussed in the analysis. The analysis has been put after the translation, rather
than prefixed as an introduction, not only because it is
longer, but also in order not to preëmpt the rightful
primacy of the text. For the analysis is designed only
as an aid, not as a substitute. The reader is therefore
urged to read the *Poetics* first and then to use the
analysis hypothetically and tentatively until he can see,
from the text itself, to what extent it can be applied.

The translation is based on the Greek text as edited
by Ingram Bywater. In the few instances in which I
have departed from his reading I have returned to the
reading of our primary source for the *Poetics*, the
eleventh-century manuscript, Parisinus 1741. In rendering Greek proper names I have with some exceptions
given them their Greek rather than Latinized spelling.
Since it is customary to refer to passages in Aristotle's
writings by the page and line on which the passage
appears in Bekker's edition of the Greek text, this pagi-
nation has been inserted in the margin of the transla-

tion. The letters "a" and "b" added to the page number indicate in which of the two columns on Bekker's page the passage is found. In translation the line numbers can, of course, be only approximate. This is important to consider when using the index.

This book has grown out of seven years teaching of the *Poetics* and the translation has gone through several revisions. There are three people for whose generous help I owe especial thanks. My greatest debt is to Prof. Richard P. McKeon, without whom this book would have been impossible. His insights and suggestions freely given over a period of many years have helped me over many problems in the interpretation of the *Poetics*. I wish also to thank my friend and colleague, Dr. James Schroeter, for the many hours in which we have puzzled over difficult passages together. His penetrating and sensitive reading of the *Poetics* has been invaluable in testing many of the ideas developed in the analysis. Lastly, to my wife, my grateful thanks for reading and rereading the manuscript in countless versions, that it might be less obscure and less demanding on the reader than the natural proclivities of my style would make it.

KENNETH A. TELFORD
June 14, 1960

Wright Jr. College, Chicago

ARISTOTLE'S POETICS

TRANSLATION

POETICS[1]

8   1. We are to speak about [1] both poetic [or productive] science[2] itself and its species, [2] what the power of each species is, [3] how plots ought
10   to be constructed if the making is to be done beautifully, and moreover [4] from how many and what sort of parts [the making ought to be constructed], and similarly about anything else that belongs to this method, first beginning, in accordance with nature, with first things.

Epic-making and the making of tragedy, and moreover comedy and the making of dithyrambs,[3]
15   as well as most of the art of the aulos and the art of the kithara,[4] all happen to be imitations, [i.e.

1. The title which the codex gives is ΠΕΡΙ ΠΟΙΗΤΙΚΗΣ and would perhaps be better translated by *Concerning The Productive* or, by implication, *Concerning Productive Science.*

2. Poetic or productive science for Aristotle covers any kind of making, including the products of both useful and fine art, but only in respect of their production, not in respect of any external criterion or purpose they might serve. A "poem" is therefore *anything* made or produced, although a poem in the most complete sense would be a literary work.

3. The dithyramb was a choral poem originally in celebration of Dionysos, accompanied by the aulos and sung by a chorus of fifty.

4. These are examples of instrumental music without words. The aulos was a flute-type instrument associated with the cult of Dionysos. The kithara was related to the lyre and associated with Apollo. Both were used in drama to accompany those portions which were sung, but especially the aulos.

it is] the composite whole[5] [that is the imitation].
But they differ from one another in three respects,
for either [1] they imitate in materials which are
different in kind, or [2] they imitate objects which
are different in kind, or [3] they imitate differently
and not in the same manner.

For just as [1] some men (either through art or
through habituation)[6] imitate many things by mak-
20 ing likenesses both in colors and in shapes, and
[2] some by means of voice,[7] so also all of the arts
mentioned produce imitation in rhythm, speech,
and harmony, either separately or mixed. For example, [a] only harmony and rhythm are used in
both the art of the aulos and the art of the kithara
25 and any others which happen to be this sort of
power, as is the art of pipers.[8] [b] The arts of

5. "Composite whole" means here, as throughout Aristotle's
writings, either the existing concrete object, i.e. a synthesis
or whole of form and matter, or the concrete process which
is this object potentially.

6. An art work can be effected either by means of a
learned rational productive faculty which constitutes an art
(see *Ethics* VI, 4) or by means of an habituation which is a
part of a man's natural abilities undirected by reason. Cf.
1451[a] 23 and *Ethics* VI, 13.

7. In the strict sense voice is the sound of an animate or
ensouled thing, and especially the sound of man which possesses significance as well. Inanimate things like musical instruments are said to have voice because, like strict voice,
their sounds have duration, melody, and timbre. See *On the
Soul*, 420[b] 5 and below 1456[b] 22. Voice in the complete sense,
therefore, has the three forms mentioned in the next clause:
rhythm, speech, and harmony. Rhythm is the form or synthesis of meter, harmony is the ratio or relationship between
either simultaneous or successive pitches, melody is the
synthesis of rhythm and harmony, and speech is voice in
respect of its significance. The Greek senses of these terms
thus do not always coincide with our English meanings.

8. The shepherd's pipe or Pan's pipe was a series of reeds
of different length bound together and sounded by blowing
across the holes as in a flute.

dancers imitate in rhythms alone without harmony, for by means of the rhythms of their figurations even dancers imitate characters, passions, and ac-

1447b tions. [c] Thus far that art happens to be nameless

8 which uses only bare[9] speech or meters, and if meters either some one kind or several kinds mixed with one another. For we would have no common

10 name for the mimes[10] of Sophron and Xenarchos and a Socratic discussion,[11] nor would we have one if the imitation were made by means of trimeters or elegiacs[12] or something else of this sort, if it were not that men connect the making of poems with the use of meter and call men elegiac poets

15 and epic poets, not by virtue of their producing an imitation, but by virtue of their common use of meter. For even if a man brings out a medical or physical treatise in meter they are accustomed to calling the man a poet. Yet there is nothing except the meter which is common to Homer and Empedokles, and on this account it is just to call the former a poet, but the latter a physicist rather than

20 a poet. In the same way, even if a man were to produce an imitation by mixing all meters, as Chairemon produced *The Centaur,* a mixed rhapsody of all meters, one must still call him a poet. Let us, therefore, determine these things in this

9. I.e. without the ornamentation of harmony.

10. A kind of drama imitative of common life and action, usually farcical and without meter.

11. Dramatic sketches comparable to Plato's dialogues about Socrates, but poetic rather than philosophic in nature and intent.

12. A plaintive song accompanied by the aulos. The verse was dactylic and in couplets which made free use of enjambment. The first line of the couplet was hexameter while the second was pentameter with a strong caesura in the third foot. In time this meter came to be used to express a wide variety of effects.

manner.[13] [d] Some arts use all of the things men-
25 tioned (by which I mean rhythm, melody, and
meter), e.g. the making of dithyrambics and the
art of nomes,[14] as well as tragedy and comedy. But
they differ in that the former use all of these materials at the same time, while the latter use them
only in various parts.

These, therefore, I call the differentiae of the
arts in respect of the materials in which the imitation is produced.

1448ª   2. Since imitators imitate agents,[15] and these of
necessity are either worthy or base (for differences
between characters are nearly always consequent
on this distinction alone, since it is in respect of
badness or virtue that all men differ in their characters), the objects imitated are either better than
5 we are, worse than we are, or such as we are, just
as with painters. For Polygnotos makes likenesses
of men better than we are, Pauson of men worse
than we are, and Dionysios of men similar to us.
And it is evident that each of the imitations spoken
of above[16] possesses these differentiae and is different by imitating objects that are different in this
manner. For even in dancing, aulos-playing, and
10 kithara-playing these dissimilarities arise, as also
in the art concerned with speeches and bare meters.
Homer, for example, imitates men better than we
are, Kleophon men similar to us, while Hegemon
of Thasos, the first to produce parodies, and Niko-
chares, who produced *The Deiliad,* imitate men
worse than we are. Similarly in the case of dithy-

13. I.e. let it be agreed that things cannot be named or
defined solely in terms of the materials from which they are
made.
14. A solo poem accompanied by the kithara.
15. For a discussion of this statement see p. 72.
16. 1447ª 14.

15 rambs and nomes, one might imitate as . . .[17] or
as in the *Cyclopses* of Timotheos and Philoxenos.
It is in respect of this differentia also that tragedy
stands apart from comedy, for the latter wishes to
imitate men worse than those of now, the former
men who are better.

3. The third differentia is the way in which one
20 might imitate each of these objects. For one may
imitate the same objects in the same materials
either [1] by narrating (and the poet can narrate
either by becoming someone else as Homer makes
his poems, or by being himself and not changing),
or [2] by imitating everyone as acting and func-
tioning.

Imitation, then, as we expressed at the begin-
25 ning, has these three differentiae: [1] the materials
in which the imitation is produced, [2] the objects
which are imitated, and [3] the way in which the
imitation is produced. Thus, in one way Sophokles
as an imitator is the same as Homer, for both
imitate the worthy, while in another way he is the
same as Aristophanes, for both imitate men as acting and doing. Hence it is, some say, that these
poems are called dramas (δράματα); because they
imitate men doing (δρᾶν). On this account, also,
30 both tragedy and comedy are claimed by the Dorians, for comedy is claimed by the Megarians (by
those here in Megara as having arisen with their
democracy, by those in Sicily because the poet
Epicharmos lived much before Chionides and
Magnes), while tragedy is claimed by some of the
35 Dorians in Peloponnesos. They make their claim
by making the names "comedy" and "tragedy"
signs [of the place where comedy and tragedy
arose]. For they say that they call their outskirts

17. The text is corrupt at this point. There may in fact
be a whole line omitted.

"hamlets" (κῶμαι) whereas Athenians call theirs
"villages" (δῆμοι), as though comedians (κωμῳδοί)
are so called, not from their revelling (κωμάζειν),
but by virtue of their wandering from hamlet to
hamlet, since they were dishonored in the town.
1448ᵇ They say also that what they call doing (δρᾶν) the
Athenians call acting (πράττειν).

Let this, therefore, suffice concerning what and
how many are the differentiae of imitation.

4. It is likely that poetic [or productive] science
5 in general was generated by two causes which are
themselves natural.[18] For [1] imitating is innate
in men from childhood. Men differ from other
animals in that they are the most imitative, and
their first learning is produced through imitation.
Again, [2] all men delight in imitations. A sign of
10 this is what happens in respect of the functions [of
imitations].[19] For we delight in contemplating the
most exact likenesses of things which are in themselves painful to see, e.g. the shapes of the most
dishonored beasts and corpses. The cause of this is
that learning is most pleasant, not only to philosophers, but to others as well, however little they
15 share in it. For men delight in seeing likenesses
because in contemplating them it happens that
they are learning and reasoning out[20] what each

18. For a discussion of this statement see p. 76.
19. The function of an imitation is the kind of pleasure
proper to it, this pleasure or affection being a quality or
form of the imitation itself. Cf. 1453ᵇ 13. "What happens
in respect of the function" is this pleasure as it arises in the
audience and becomes an emotion in the psychological sense.
This audience reaction, however, can only be a sign or symp-
tom of the quality or form of the art work since it is an
effect of that form, not its principle or cause. Arguments from
signs are from effects to causes and more persuasive than
demonstrative. Cf. 1453ᵃ 26.
20. For a discussion of the meaning of learning in connection with imitations see p. 76.

thing is, e.g. that this man [in the painting] is that [sort of man]; for if by fortune one has not previously seen what is imitated, the likeness will not produce pleasure as an imitation, but because of its execution, or surface coloring, or some other
20 cause of this sort.[21] Imitating, then, is in accordance with our nature, as also are harmony and rhythm (for it is apparent that meters are parts of rhythms[22]), and from this natural beginning, advancing mostly by small steps, men generated [the process of] making out of their improvisations.

[The process of] making then broke up into kinds in accordance with the appropriate charac-
25 ters of the poets. For the more dignified poets imitated noble actions and the actions of noble men, while the more trivial poets imitated the actions of base men, producing invectives at first as the former produced hymns and encomia. While, then, we have no poems imitative of the base by poets before Homer, though it is likely there were many,
30 we do have some beginning with Homer, e.g. his *Margites* and others of this sort. In these invectives poets came to use iambic meter by virtue of its suitability, and hence such meter is now called iambic ($\iota\alpha\mu\beta\epsilon\hat{\iota}o\nu$) in that poets lampooned ($\iota\alpha\mu$-$\beta\ell\zeta\omega$) one another in this meter. And so, some of the ancients came to produce heroic poems and others lampoons. And just as Homer was the most
35 important poet of the worthy (because he not only

21. The pleasure that constitutes the function of an imitation thus derives not only from its organization as determined by the thing imitated (the formal cause of the genesis of the art). but from the execution or manner of imitation (the efficient cause), as well as from the medium of imitation such as color (the material cause).

22. Rhythm is to meter as melody is to harmony, i.e. form to matter; for in each pair the former is the immediate organizing form, while the latter is a material of that organization.

produced these well, but also in dramatic imitation), so also he was the first to show the patterns of comedy by producing dramatically,[23] not an invective, but an imitation of the ludicrous. For 1449ᵃ his *Margites* in relation to comedies is analogous to his *Iliad* and *Odyssey* in relation to tragedies. When tragedy and comedy had appeared, then, poets turned to each kind of making by virtue of its appropriate nature, some becoming poets of 5 comedy instead of lampoons, others teachers of tragedy[24] instead of epics, because the patterns of the later arts were greater and more honored than those of the earlier.[25]

Now to examine whether or not tragedy in its forms is now adequate,[26] and to judge this both in itself essentially and in relation to the specta-

23. "Dramatically" here means that the incidents receive their synthesis (plot) through their imitation of action rather than suffering, character, or spectacle. Cf. 1455ᵇ 32ff. The reference (as in 1459ᵃ 19) is to the thing imitated, not the manner of imitation.

24. The tragic poet was called a "teacher" of his art because of the fact that he trained the chorus and actors.

25. From a poetic or productive point of view there is no meaning to the question of which is the better of two different kinds of art. A good poem is simply one that is well made —that is, one that effects its proper pleasure through an appropriate implementation of its parts. Where the pleasure of two works differs in kind no poetic comparison can be made between their organizations. The comparison here, as well as that between epic and tragedy in chapters 23-26, is possible only because the functions or proper pleasures of the arts compared are the same in kind.

26. Poetic science gets its subject matter as an historically given fact, as this chapter indicates. What the nature of a genre is is given to the inquirer, and his poetic task is simply to discover the unity and interrelation of parts that the art object already possesses. To "judge" this object is to apply some criterion external to it for purposes which can no longer be productive. Cf. 1451ᵃ 6 where Aristotle again rejects external criteria for the solution of poetic problems.

tors, belongs to another discussion. Tragedy, therefore, as well as comedy, having arisen at the begin-
10 ning through improvisations (the former due to
the leaders of the dithyramb, the latter due to the
leaders of the phallic songs which even today are
continued by custom in many of our cities), then
grew by small steps, advancing until it became
what it appears today. And tragedy went through
15 many changes, stopping when it had attained its
nature. [1] First Aeschylos brought the number of
performers[27] from one to two, lessened the [num-
ber of melodies] of the chorus, and rendered
speech the primary contestant.[28] Sophokles then
brought the number of performers to three and
introduced scene painting. Moreover, [2] the mag-
20 nitude, from small plots and ludicrous diction, by
changing from satyric art, became at length dignified, while the meter, from tetrameter,[29] came to
be iambic.[30] For while the first poems used tetrameter because the making was satyric and more involved with dancing, when diction had arisen
nature itself discovered the appropriate meter, for

27. The number of performers used in a play was not the
same as the number of characters represented, since one
performer might, at different times, take the parts of several
characters. The number of performers simply limited the
number of speaking characters on the stage at one time.

28. Greek plays were presented in competitions or contests,
and prizes were awarded to the victors. By extension the
performers and even parts of the play were also called "con-
testants." Cf. 1456ᵃ 26.

29. Tetrameter is short for trochaic tetrameter. However,
the Greeks considered two trochees as constituting one fòot.
A verse in trochaic tetrameter would thus have eight rather
than four trochees.

30. Iambic trimeter was the customary metrical form for
the episodes of both tragedy and comedy though there are
numerous exceptions to this, especially in comedy. As with
trochees, two iambs were considered as constituting a foot.

25 the iambic is the most speakable of meters. There is a sign of this, for it is iambic we speak most in discourse with one another, while hexameters[31] are seldom spoken even when we depart from the harmony of common speech. Moreover, [3] the
28 number of episodes was increased. As to the other
30 things which are said to ornament tragedy, and how each was introduced, let it suffice that we have mentioned them, for perhaps it would be a great deal of work to go through the particulars.

5. Comedy, as we have mentioned,[32] is an imitation of the more base, not, however, in respect of every kind of badness, but in respect of that part of the ugly which is ludicrous. For the ludi-
35 crous is that sort of mistake or ugliness which is painless and not destructive, e.g. the ludicrous mask is something ugly and distorted but without pain. While, therefore, the changes and the poets through whom these changes came about are not forgotten in the case of tragedy, those of comedy
1449b have been forgotten because at the beginning it was not assumed to be worthy. It was a long time before the archon permitted a chorus of comedians, the performers up to that time having volunteered. Those who are called poets of comedy are remembered only as far back as when comedy already possessed certain patterns. Who it was who
5 gave comedy masks, or prologues, or many performers and such is not known. But the making of plots came at the beginning from Sicily with Epicharmos and Phormis, while of those in Athens Krates first began to discard the form of the lampoon to produce universal arguments[33] and plots.

31. Hexameter is short for dactylic hexameter, otherwise known as heroic meter, and was the standard meter for epics.
32. 1448ᵃ 16.
33. For the meaning of "universal argument" see 1455ᵃ 34ff.

While, therefore, epic-making follows tragedy as
10 far as being an imitation of the worthy made from
majestic meter only, they differ [1] in that epic-
making has simple meter[34] and is narrative. They
differ, moreover, [2] in length, in that tragedy tries
to stay within a single circuit of the sun or alters
but little from this, while epic-making is indeter-
15 minate in respect of time, although the first tragedies and epics were made similarly in this respect.
And [3] while some of their parts are the same,
some are proper to tragedy, and on this account
whoever knows what is worthy or base concerning
tragedy knows this also concerning epic. For while
the parts which epic-making possesses are attributes of tragedy as well, not all the parts of trag-
20 edy are in epic-making.[35]

6. Of imitative art in hexameter and of comedy,
therefore, we will speak later.[36] Let us now speak
of tragedy, gathering up the definition of its substance as it has arisen from what we have expressed.

Tragedy, therefore, is imitation of worthy and   ✓
25 complete action having magnitude, in speech made
pleasing with each form [of pleasing ornamenta-
tion] used separately in the parts of tragedy, performed and not produced through narration,
achieving through pity and fear a catharsis of such
affections. By speech made pleasing I mean speech
which possesses rhythm, harmony, and melody. By
30 forms used separately I mean that some parts are
achieved through meter only while others are
achieved through melody.

34. By simple Aristotle means plain or without the ornamentation of harmony.
35. Cf. 1459[b] 9-16.
36. Imitation in hexameter (i.e. epic-making) is compared
with tragedy in chapters 23-26. Aristotle is supposed to have
treated of comedy in a book now lost.

Since agents [rather than the poet] produce the imitation, first, of necessity, [1] one part of tragedy will be the ornament of spectacle, and second, [2] the making of melody and [3] diction, since the agents produce the imitation in these materials.

35 By diction I mean the synthesis of the meters; by the making of melody I mean that power which is apparent to all. But tragedy is an imitation of ac-ʰions acted by certain agents who of necessity are of a certain kind by virtue of character and

1450ᵃ thought, for it is because of these that we say that actions are of a certain kind, these two, character and thought, being the natural causes of actions,[37] and it is by virtue of these that all agents happen to be fortunate or unfortunate. Therefore, while [4] plot is the imitation of action, for I mean by

5 plot the synthesis of the incidents, [5] characters are the things by virtue of which we say the agents are of a certain kind, and [6] thought exists in whatever they say when demonstrating something or declaring some consideration. Of necessity, therefore, every tragedy has six parts by virtue of which tragedy is a certain kind of thing. These

10 are plot, characters, diction, thought, spectacle, and the making of melody. For two of these parts are the materials in which the agents imitate, one is how they imitate, three are the things that they imitate, and besides these there are no others. Those agents who have used these forms have not, we may say, been few, for every tragedy has specta-cles, character, plot, diction, melody, and thought.

15 The greatest of these is the construction of the

37. It is in *nature* that character and thought determine action. See *Ethics*, II, 2, 1104ᵃ 27-ᵇ3. In *art*, as the next two paragraphs argue, since it is action that is imitated, characters will be determined by the requirements of that action, and thought will be determined both by the character who ex-presses it and the action in which he is involved.

incidents, for [1] tragedy is imitation, not of men, but of action or life, of happiness [and misery; and happiness] and misery exist in action, and the end of life is a certain action, not a quality. It is by virtue of their characters that agents are of a
20   certain kind, but it is by virtue of their actions that they are happy or the contrary. Therefore, just as agents do not act in order to imitate characters, but rather their characters are included at the same time because of the actions, so also the incidents and the plot are the end of tragedy, the end being the greatest of all parts. Moreover, [2] without action the tragedy would not arise, but it
25   might arise without characters. For the tragedies of most of the young poets are characterless, and in general many poets produce imitations of this sort. For example, among painters, Zeuxis suffers in relation to Polygnotos, for Polygnotos is a good painter of character, while none of the paintings of Zeuxis include character. Moreover, [3] if one were to place together successive expressions which
30   involve characters and are well made in respect of diction and thought, one might produce the function of tragedy, but one would produce this much more with a tragedy which, though wanting in these respects, has plot or a construction of incidents. And in addition, the greatest parts by which tragedy attracts the soul, the reversals and recognitions, are parts of the plot. Moreover, [4] a sign
35   tions, are parts of the plot. Moreover, [4] a sign [of the importance of plot] is that those attempting to produce tragedies are able to make exact diction and characters before they are able to construct the incidents, e.g. nearly all of the first poets.

Plot, therefore, is the principle and, as it were, the soul of tragedy, while characters are second. For
1450b in the art of painting the case is nearly the same, since the most beautiful dyes poured on in a flood would not give the enjoyment of a likeness drawn

in chalk. Tragedy is then an imitation of action,
and mainly because of this an imitation of agents.
5 Third is thought, which is being able to say what
may be or is suitable and is that aspect of speeches
which is the function of politics and rhetoric. For
the ancient poets made their characters speak po-
litically, the present ones make them speak rhetor-
ically. Character is what makes the choice evident
—that is, what sort of action is chosen or avoided
in cases not evident in themselves—and on this
account those speeches do not possess character
10 which do not in a general way include what the
speaker chooses or avoids.[38] Thought exists in
those speeches in which the speakers demonstrate
that something is or is not the case or declare
something universal.[39] Fourth is the diction of the
speeches. By diction I mean, as was said before,[40]
the interpretation [of things] through language,
15 this being the same power in meters and in
speeches. Of the remaining parts the making of
melody is the most important of the pleasing accessories, while spectacle, though it attracts the
soul, is the most inartistic and least appropriate
to poetic science. For the power of tragedy is possible even without a contest and performers, and
moreover, the execution of spectacles more authori-
20 tatively belongs to the art of the costume-maker
than to that of the poet.

38. That is, character is a moral habit, and to show character the speech must show the moral choice as an example
of a general tendency. Unless this obtains there is character
in name only. Cf. 1450ᵃ 24.
39. Thus, just as there may be speeches (expressive of
thought) which do not exhibit character, so there may be
diction which does not exhibit thought.
40. 1449ᵇ 34. Aristotle thus implies that to synthesize meters
is to establish relations between words and this constitutes
the interpretation of what the words signify. Cf. the definition
of metaphor, 1457ᵇ 6.

7. Having determined the parts, let us now speak of what sort the construction of the incidents ought to be, since this is what is primary and most important in tragedy. We have assumed that tragedy is imitation of action that is complete

25 and whole and has a certain magnitude, for a whole may exist without possessing magnitude.

A whole is that which has a beginning, a middle, and a completion. A beginning is that which is not itself of necessity after something else, but after which something else naturally exists or comes to be. A completion is the contrary of this, being that which itself naturally exists or comes

30 to be, either of necessity or for the most part, after something else, but after which there is nothing. A middle is that which is itself after some other thing and after which there is also something else. A well constructed plot, therefore, ought not to begin or complete itself wherever it may happen to, but ought to use the forms just mentioned.

Moreover, what is beautiful (not only an ani-

35 mal, but anything constructed of parts) ought to have not only ordered parts, but also a magnitude which does not merely happen to be attributed of it. For the beautiful exists in magnitude as well as in order, and on this account neither a very small animal nor a very great one comes to be beautiful. For in the case of the former the contemplation becomes confused by arising in a nearly imperceptible length of time, while in the case of

1451ᵃ the latter (e.g. if the animal had a length of ten thousand stadia), the contemplation does not all arise together, and the unity and the whole of the thing contemplated escapes from the contemplation. Thus, just as bodies and animals ought to have magnitude, this being what is easily seen all

5 together, so plot ought to have length, this being what is easily remembered. What the limit of

length ought to be relative to a contest and its perception [by spectators] does not belong to art, for if there had to be a hundred tragedies contested the contests would be timed by water clocks, as now and again men say they ought to be. As to
10 a limit according with the nature of the thing itself, however (while always, the greater the length, as long as all of it is evident together, the more beautiful it is in respect of magnitude), we can determine this simply[41] by saying as much magnitude as is in accordance with what is likely or necessary in an arising succession of incidents which happen to change from misfortune to good fortune or from good fortune to misfortune, this be-
15 ing an adequate limit to magnitude.

8. A plot is not a unity, as some suppose, by being about one agent, for many and indefinite things happen to one agent, some of which do not make a unity. So also the actions of one agent are many, and from them no unity of action arises.
20 On this account it is likely that all those poets were mistaken who produced *Herakleids* or *Theseids* or such poems, for they supposed that since Herakles was one the plot was also one. It is likely also that Homer, either through art or nature, knew this well, just as he differed in other respects.
25 For in producing the *Odyssey* he did not make it concern all that happened to Odysseus, e.g. his being wounded on Parnassos or pretending to be mad when the call to arms was given, incidents of which it is neither necessary nor likely that one arise with the rise of the other. Instead he constructed the *Odyssey*, and similarly the *Iliad*,

41. I.e. without qualification or in itself, and not with reference to criteria external to poetic purposes.

30 around one action in the sense we mean.[42] Therefore, as in other imitative arts one imitation is of
one thing, so also plot, since it is imitation of action, ought to be imitation of action that is one
and whole, and the parts of the incidents ought to
be constructed in such a way that when the parts
are replaced or removed the whole is dislocated
35 and moved. For that whose presence or absence
makes nothing evident is no part of the whole.

9. It is also apparent from what has been mentioned that the function of the poet is not to
speak of incidents which have come to be, but
rather of incidents which might come to be, i.e.
what are possible by virtue of either the likely or
1451^b the necessary. For the historian and the poet do
not differ in speaking in meters or without meters,
since even if the histories of Herodotos were put
into meters they would nonetheless be history,
either with meters or without. Rather they differ
in this, that while the former speaks of incidents
5 that have come to be, the latter speaks of incidents that might come to be. On this account [the
process of] making is both more philosophic and
more worthy than history, for making speaks more
of universals while history speaks more of particulars. The universal, being that which characters of
a certain kind happen to say or do in accordance
with what is likely or necessary in a certain kind
10 of succession of incidents, is that at which [the
process of] making aims in setting down names for
characters, while the particular is what Alkibiades,
for example, did or suffered.
Now in respect of comedy this has already become evident, for having constructed the plot in

42. The action is unified or one if the incidents are likely
or necessary. 1450^b 27, 1451^a 12, 27. Also below, *passim.*

this way through likelihoods, they assume whatever names they happen to assume and do not, as
did the poets of the lampoons, make the plot con-
15 cern particular names. In respect of tragedy, however, they cling to the names of men who lived.
The cause of this is that whatever is possible is
persuasive. Therefore, while we do not as yet be-
lieve that those incidents are possible which have
not come to be, it is apparent that incidents which
have arisen are possible, for an incident does not
arise if it is impossible. Nevertheless, in some
20 tragedies though there are one or two known
names the others are made up, while in other tragedies none are known, e.g. in Agathon's *Antheus*,
for in this tragedy both incidents and names are
made up and it gives enjoyment nonetheless. Thus
the poet must not seek to cling altogether to the
traditional plots with which our tragedies are con-
25 cerned. Indeed, it is ludicrous to seek to do this,
since even the known plots are known only to a
few and yet give enjoyment to all alike. It is evident from these things, therefore, that the poet
ought to be more a poet of plots than of meters,
inasmuch as he is a poet by virtue of his imitation
and it is actions that he imitates. And even if he
30 happens to produce incidents that have arisen, he
is nonetheless a poet, for nothing prevents some
incidents which have arisen from being the sort of
incidents that are likely or possible, and it is in
respect of this aspect of incidents that he is a poet.

Of simple plots and actions the worst are the
episodic. By an episodic plot I mean a plot in
35 which the episodes follow one another with neither
likelihood nor necessity. Such plots are produced
by base poets because of themselves, while good
poets produce them because of the performers,
for in producing them for competitions and in

extending the plot beyond its potentiality they
1452ª often find it necessary to distort the succession of
incidents.

Yet the imitation is noT only of a complete
action, but also of fearsome and piteous incidents,
and incidents come to be most fearsome and
piteous, or more so, when they arise because of
one another and yet are contrary to what would
5 seem to follow. For the wondrous will be more
wondrous if it arises in this way than if it comes to
be through chance or fortune, since even incidents
which come to be through fortune seem to be most
wondrous to the extent that they appear to arise
purposely, e.g. as the statue of Mitys at Argos
killed the man who caused Mitys' death by falling
on him while he was contemplating it, for such
10 incidents do not seem to arise without plan. Thus
of necessity plots of this sort are the most beautiful.

10. Some plots are simple while others are complex, for the actions, of which the plots are imitations, have these [two forms] directly attributed
of them since they are of these kinds. By simple
15 I mean action which arises continuously and is
unified in the way defined 43 but in which change
arises without reversal or recognition. By complex
I mean action in which change arises with either
recognition or reversal or both. These ought to
arise from the construction of the plot itself, so
that they arise, either of necessity or as a likeli-
20 hood, out of what happens to have previously
arisen, for it makes a great difference whether this
incident arises because of that incident or after it.

11. A reversal, as we have mentioned,44 is a
43. See footnote 42.
44. 1451ª 12.

change to the contrary of previous actions,[45] and
this, as we said, in accordance with likelihood or
25   necessity. Thus in the *Oedipus* the messenger,
coming to gladden Oedipus and rid him of his
fear concerning his mother, produces the contrary
by making it evident who Oedipus is.[46] Again, in
the *Lynkeus*,[47] as Lynkeus is being led to his
death with Danaos following to kill him, from the
previous actions it happens that Danaos is killed
and he is saved.

30   A recognition, as the name signifies, is a change
from ignorance to knowledge, and so to either
friendship or enmity in those determined to good
fortune or misfortune. Recognition is most beautiful when it arises at the same time as reversal, as
does the recognition in the *Oedipus*.[48] There are
also other recognitions, for what we have men-
35   tioned happens even in respect of inanimate things
or whatever there may happen to be. One may also
recognize whether something has or has not been
done. But that which most belongs to plot, as well
as action, is that which we have mentioned,[49] for
this sort of recognition and reversal will possess
1452[b]   either pity or fear and we have assumed that tragedy is imitation of such actions.[50] Moreover, it is
in respect of such actions that one happens to be
fortunate and unfortunate. Since, then, recogni-

45. A reversal is thus an action, not a suffering. Cf. 1452[b] 11.
That is, it is a misfortune the protagonist brings upon himself and not one caused by another.

46. *Oedipus the King* by Sophokles, 925ff.

47. By Theodektes. Cf. 1455[b] 29.

48. The recognition is finally completed at the end of the
fourth episode, 1182, and with this knowledge the banishment
ordered by Oedipus proves to be his own.

49. I.e. recognition of a character. This changes the passions of the one who makes the recognition since what is
recognized is the friendship or enmity of that character.

50. I.e. in the definition of tragedy, 1449[b] 27.

tion is recognition of certain characters, sometimes
only one character is recognized by another, it
5 being already evident who the latter is, while sometimes there ought to be a recognition of both, as
Iphigenia is recognized by Orestes through the
sending of the letter,[51] but another recognition is
needed to make Orestes known to Iphigenia.[52]

Two parts of plot, therefore, reversal and recog-
10 nition, are concerned with these things. A third
part is suffering. Reversal and recognition having
already been mentioned, suffering is destructive
or painful action such as the appearance [on stage]
of death, severe pain, woundings, and such.

12. The parts of tragedy which ought to be used
15 as forms [of a tragedy as a whole] we have already
mentioned.[53] On the other hand, the quantitative
parts into which a tragedy is separately divided
are these: prologue, episode, exode, choral part,
and the parts of the latter, the parode and stasimon, these two being common to all tragedies,
while melodies from the stage and dirges are
proper to some only. A prologue is the whole [or
20 unified] part of a tragedy before the parode of the
chorus. An episode is the whole part of a tragedy
which is between whole choral melodies. An exode
is the whole part of a tragedy after which there is
no melody of the chorus. Of the choral parts a
parode is the whole of the first diction of the
chorus, a stasimon is a melody of the chorus without anapests or trochees, while a dirge is a lamen-
25 tation common to the chorus and the performers
on the stage. The parts of tragedy to be used [as
forms of tragedy as a whole] having been men-

51. *Iphigenia in Tauris* by Euripides, 769-786.
52. *Ibid.*, 800-830.
53. The formal parts are the six parts given in chapter 6

tioned, these are the quantitative parts into which a tragedy is separately divided.

13. After the things we have now expressed we must next speak of the things at which one ought to aim, which ought to be well conceived when 30 plots are constructed, and from which the function of tragedy will arise.[54]

Since, therefore, the synthesis of the most beautiful tragedy ought to be, not simple, but complex, and imitative of things fearsome and piteous[55] (for this is proper to this kind of imitation), it is evident, first, that what ought to appear in tragedy 35 is not [1] equitable men[56] changing from good fortune to misfortune, for this is neither fearsome nor piteous, but repulsive. Nor [2] wicked men changing from the lack of fortune to good fortune, for this is the most untragic of all, since it possesses nothing which tragedy ought to have, being nei- 1453ᵃ ther humane[57] nor piteous nor fearsome. Nor [3] exceedingly villainous men falling from good for-

54. The function of tragedy is its proper pleasure, i.e. the catharsis of pity and fear. See 1449ᵇ 27 and 1453ᵇ 11 and pp. 106–9.

55. The criterion which guides the discussion is thus no longer likelihood and necessity but pity and fear. The reference to beauty shows that beauty has not only a structural aspect (as stated at 1450ᵇ 34), but also an affective or functional aspect.

56. The equitable man has the highest of all moral virtues. Justice expressed in a law always produces some inequities because of its universality. The equitable man is the one who goes beyond the letter of the law to conform to its spirit when the letter and the spirit clash, especially when the letter of the law would be to his advantage. Equity is thus the correction of justice. See *Ethics* V, 10.

57. The humane or philanthropic means for Aristotle anything befitting or appropriate to human values. It is not simply the indiscriminately benevolent. Cf. the use of the term in the next sentence. Its contrary appears to be the repulsive mentioned in the previous sentence.

tune to misfortune, for while this kind of construction is humane, it possesses neither pity nor fear.
For the former concerns misfortunes that are un-
5 deserved, while the latter concerns misfortunes
that are similar [to what previous incidents make
possible]. That is, pity concerns the undeserved,
while fear concerns the similar.[58] What happens
in these cases, then, will be neither piteous nor
fearsome. What remains, therefore, [4] is something in between.[59] This is the sort of man who
does not differ in virtue or justice, and who
changes to misfortune, not because of badness or
10 wickedness, but because of some mistake,[60] he being a man held in high opinion and of good fortune, e.g. Oedipus, or Thyestes, and notable men
of such families.

It is necessary, therefore, that the beautiful plot
be single rather than double,[61] as some say, and
change, not from misfortune to good fortune, but
15 the contrary, from good fortune to misfortune,[62]

58. Pity and fear are thus defined as the functional properties of the dramatic action, not as emotional effects in the
audience.

59. I.e. a character neither equitable nor *exceedingly* villainous, but having average virtues. He may, however, be
moderately villainous (as is Medea) provided he has other
virtues which make his actions piteous and fearsome. Cf.
1456^a 21.

60. In the most complete sense the tragic mistake or hamartia (literally, a missing of the mark), as Aristotle himself
indicates throughout chapter 14, is an action, not a suffering
or a flaw of character. The latter two senses may also be
present, but in themselves they are incomplete senses of
hamartia as Aristotle conceives it. See p. 123.

61. See below, 1453^a 30.

62. As long as Aristotle is considering the reversal in itself
alone, the direction of the change must be from good fortune
to bad to be tragic. But since catharsis can be effected through
recognition without reversal (1152^a 16 and 1454^a 4-9) the
change, in general, may go in either direction. Cf. 1451^a 13,
1452^a 31, and 1455^b 28. See also pp. 106ff.

not through wickedness, but through the great mistake of a man who is either such as we have mentioned or better rather than worse. The tragedies which have arisen are a sign of this, for at first poets recounted whatever plots they happened to recount, but now they synthesize their most beautiful tragedies about a few households, e.g. those
20 of Alkmaion, Oedipus, Orestes, Meleager, Thyestes, Telephos, and any others who happened to suffer or produce terrible things. That tragedy, therefore, which is the most beautiful by virtue of art arises from such a construction. On this account, also, those are mistaken who blame Euri-
25 pides because he does this in his tragedies and completes many of them in misfortune. For this, as we mentioned, is the right sort of completion. And there is the greatest sign that this is so, for on the stages and in the contests those which are of this kind, if rightly done, appear to be the most tragic,[63] and Euripides, even if he does not man-
30 age other things well, still appears to be the most tragic of poets. Second to this is that construction which some say comes first, i.e. the plot which has a double construction, as does the *Odyssey,* and is completed in contrary fortunes for the better and the worse. This seems to be first because of the weakness of the spectators, for the poets merely
35 follow and make the plot in accordance with the petition of the spectators. But the pleasure of this is not that of tragedy, but rather that which is appropriate to comedy, for there the greatest enemies of the plot, e.g. Orestes and Aigisthos, having at the completion become friends, withdraw, and no one is killed by anyone.

1453ᵇ   14. Now the fearsome and the piteous may arise from the spectacle, but they may also arise from

63. See footnote 19.

the construction of the incidents itself, and this way is prior and belongs to the better poet. For the plot ought to be constructed so that, even
5 without seeing the incidents arise, those who hear them will shudder and pity because of what happens, these indeed being what one would suffer upon hearing the plot of the *Oedipus*. To render this through spectacle is more inartistic and needs the office of the choregos.[64] Those who render through spectacle, not the fearsome, but only the
10 monstrous, have no share in tragedy, for one ought to seek in tragedy, not every pleasure, but that which is appropriate.[65] Since, then, it is through imitation that the poet ought to bring about the pleasure which comes from pity and fear, it is apparent that this pleasure must be produced in the incidents.[66] We must grasp, therefore, among the
15 things that befall us, what sort those are which appear terrible or grievous.

In actions of this kind it is necessary that the agents be either friends of one another, or enemies, or neither of these. Now if enemy does something to enemy there is nothing piteous, either in his producing or his being about to produce suffering, except the suffering in itself.[67] Nor is there anything piteous when the two are neither friends

64. The choregos was the one who defrayed the cost of the performance.

65. See footnote 54.

66. This statement shows as clearly as any other that the function or proper pleasure of tragedy, i.e. the catharsis of pity and fear, is essentially conceived by Aristotle as an attribute of tragedy itself, not as the emotional consequence in the audience.

67. Volition is the essence of an action (*Ethics* III, 1). Unless what is willed in an action proves contrary to what the agent wills in general, the action cannot in itself, as action, be piteous. The disclosure that one has harmed what one loves constitutes the tragic recognition, i.e. the *re*-awareness of values lost sight of, not a new discovery. See p. 105.

20   nor enemies. But sufferings which arise in friend-
ships, as when killing or something else of this
sort is either done or about to be done by brother
to brother, son to father, mother to son, or son to
mother, these the poet ought to seek. The plots
which have been handed down, therefore, are not
to be relinquished. I mean, for example, the slay-
ing of Klytaimnestra by Orestes and of Eriphyle
25   by Alkmaion; yet the poet himself ought to discover and use these traditional plots beautifully.

But what we mean by beautifully we must express more distinctly. For the action may arise with
the agent knowing and aware of what he does, as
the ancients made it arise and as Euripides also
made Medea kill her children.[68] The agent may
30   also do it while ignorant of his doing something
terrible and afterwards recognize his friendship
[to the one on whom he acts], as does Oedipus in
the tragedy by Sophokles. In this tragedy, however,
the action is external to the drama. An example
of an action that is in the tragedy itself is that of
Alkmaion in Astydamas' tragedy or that of Tele-
gonos in the *Wounded Odysseus*. Moreover, a third
35   way besides these is to be about to make some ir-
remediable action because of ignorance but to
recognize the friendship before making it. And
besides these there is no other way, for it is necessary that the action be either done or not done
and either knowingly or not knowingly. Of these,
[1] the worst is to be about to do the action knowingly and yet not do it, for this is repulsive and
not tragic since it is without suffering. On this ac-
1454ª   count no one makes tragedies in this way, or at
least seldom, as in the case of Haimon's action
toward Kreon in the *Antigone*.[69] Second, [2] is to
do the action [knowingly]. Better still, [3] is to do

68. 1236-1278.
69. By Sophokles, 1231-1240.

it in ignorance and to recognize [the friendship]
upon doing it. For there is nothing repulsive here
and the recognition is astounding. But [4] the best
5   is the last. In the *Kresphontes*, for example, Mer-
ope, being about to kill her son, does not kill him,
but instead recognizes him. In the *Iphigenia* also,
the sister recognizes her brother and does not kill
him, and in the *Helle* the son, being about to give
up his mother, recognizes her. It is because of this,
as we mentioned above,[70] that tragedies are not
10   concerned with many families. For in seeking it
was not by art but by fortune that poets discovered
the kind of incidents to render in their plots. They
therefore found it necessary to imitate those households in which sufferings of this sort have happened.

Concerning the construction of the incidents
15   and of what sort the plots ought to be, then, what
has been expressed is adequate.

15. There are four things concerning characters
which the poet ought to aim at. One of these, and
that which is primary, is that the characters be
[dramatically good or] effective.[71] There will be
character, as we said,[72] if the speech or action
makes it apparent that the agent has made a
choice, and the character is effective if this choice
20   is effective. Each kind of character may be effective, for both woman and slave may be effective
[or good for dramatic purposes] even though one
is perhaps inferior[73] and the other generally base.

70. 1453ᵃ 17-22.
71. For an explanation of these four aspects of character
see pp. 111–3.
72. 1450ᵇ 9.
73. The inferiority of the female to the male was not considered by Aristotle to be natural in the biological or psychological sense, but rather natural in terms of the function she
has in political society.

Second is that the characters be suitable, for the character may be courageous,[74] but being courageous or clever is not suitable to being womanly. Third is that the character be similar [to what the dramatic situation makes likely], for this is differ-
25 ent from making the character effective or suitable as these have been expressed. Fourth is that the character be consistent [throughout the tragedy], for even if the poet who supplies the imitation assumes a character which is inconsistent, nevertheless, such a character ought to be consistently inconsistent. There is an example of villainy not necessary [to the character's effectiveness], e.g. Menelaos in the *Orestes;*[75] of a character that is
30 unfitting and unsuitable, e.g. the lamentation of Odysseus in the *Skylla* as well as the words expressed by Melanippe; and of an inconsistent character, e.g. Iphigenia in *Iphigenia in Aulis,* for Iphigenia supplicating is not like Iphigenia later on.[76]

The poet ought always to seek what is necessary or likely in characters as well as in the construc-
35 tion of the incidents, so that it is either necessary or likely that such a character say or do such things as well as necessary or likely that this incident arise with that one. It is apparent, therefore, that the solutions of plots ought to happen as a result
1454b of the plots themselves, and not from a contrivance as in the *Medea* or as in those incidents in the

74. The Greek word for courageous is derived from the word for man and can also be translated as manly or manlike. In the fullest sense according to Aristotle courage is the fortitude with which a man faces imminent and noble death. See *Ethics* III, 6.

75. By Euripides, 682-715. The villainous choice of Menelaos has no bearing on subsequent incidents.

76. By Euripides. Cf. 1211-1252 with 1368-1403.

Iliad concerned with the embarkation.[77] The contrivance[78] should rather be used only in connection with incidents external to the drama, either
those which arise before [the incidents of the plot]
and which are not the kind a man would know,
5 or those arising later which need foretelling or
announcement, for it is to gods that we give the
[power of] seeing all. There should be nothing unreasonable in the incidents, or if there is, it should
be external to the tragedy, as in the case of the
Oedipus by Sophokles.[79]

And since tragedy is imitation of those who are
10 better, we ought to imitate good portrait painters,
for even in giving men their proper shape and in
making the imitation similar [to them] they paint
them more beautiful [than they are]. So also the
poet, when imitating irascible or easy-tempered
men or men who have such characters by having
other qualities of this sort, ought to make them
equitable as well, as for example the Achilleus of
15 Agathon and that of Homer.

These things, then, ought to be watched closely,
and in addition, those things in poetic science
which of necessity are consequent to the perception of tragedy, for one may often be mistaken
also in respect of its perception. But these things
have been adequately expressed in published discussions.

77. *Medea,* 1317, and *Iliad,* II, 155. In one case a king, in
the other a goddess, intervenes to solve the problem of the
plot.
78. Literally, the contrivance was a machine which lowered
a god into the scene to unravel the dramatic problem. Figura-
tively, it is the introduction of any character or agency external to the situation for this purpose.
79. Cf. 1460ᵃ 30.

16. What recognition is has been mentioned
above.[80] The forms of recognition are, first, that
which is most inartistic and used mostly because
of difficulties [in synthesizing the incidents], recognitions through signs. Of these some are innate,
e.g. "the lance which the Earthborn bear" or the
stars in the *Thyestes* by Karkinos, while others are
acquired. Of the latter some are in the body, e.g.
scars, while others are external, e.g. necklaces or
such things as the skiff used in the *Tyro*. But even
signs may be used in a better or worse way: e.g.
Odysseus is recognized through his scar in one way
by the nurse and in another by the swineherds.[81]
For signs which exist only for the sake of the resulting beliefs are more inartistic, as indeed are
all recognitions of this kind, while those signs
which arise from the reversal are better, e.g. the
sign which arose in the washing by the nurse.

A second form of recognition are those made
up by the poet [rather than produced by the inci-
dents] and which are on this account inartistic,
e.g. the recognition of Orestes in the *Iphigenia*
when Iphigenia recognizes that he is Orestes. For
Iphigenia is recognized by Orestes through the letter,[82] but he is recognized by Iphigenia when he
speaks, not what the plot requires, but what the
poet wishes him to say.[83] On this account such a
recognition is something close to the mistake mentioned above, for he might as well have brought
some signs. Also in the *Tereus* by Sophokles there
is the "voice" of the shuttle.

80. 1452ᵃ 29.
81. Cf. *Odyssey,* XIX, 386ff., and XXI, 205ff. The nurse's
recognition is better because she sees the scar as the likely
consequence of previous incidents. The swineherds are simply
shown the scar by Odysseus.
82. 769-786.
83. 800-830.

A third form of recognition is that through
memory, where something is known through per-
ceiving something else, e.g. in *The Cyprians* by
Dikaiogenos, for on seeing the painting he wept,
and in the story of Alkinos,[84] for on hearing the
kithara player he remembered and burst into tears,
and from these memories they were recognized.

A fourth form of recognition is that through
reasoning: e.g. in *The Libation-Bearers*[85] the reasoning is that someone similar [to Elektra] has
come, but there is no one but Orestes who is similar, therefore he has come. There is also the recognition given by Polyidos the sophist for the *Iphigenia,* for it is likely that Orestes would reason
that, since his sister was sacrified, it happens that
he himself is to be sacrificed. And in the *Tydeus*
by Theodektes, in coming to find his son, Tydeus
reasons that he himself is to be slain; while in *The
Phineidai,* on seeing the place, they reasoned out
their destiny—that they were destined to die in
that place since they had also been exposed there.
One may also synthesize the plot from the misreasoning of another [character], e.g. in *Odysseus the
False Messenger,* for he said that he would know
the bow which he had not seen, but misreasoning
is produced when there is a recognition because
of this [statement].

But of all forms of recognition the best is that
which arises from the incidents themselves, the
astonishment coming to pass through likelihoods,
e.g. the recognition in the *Oedipus* by Sophokles[86]
and that in the *Iphigenia,*[87] since it is likely that
she would wish to send a letter. For only such
recognitions as these arise without making signs

84. *Odyssey*, VIII, 521ff.
85. By Aeschylos, 168-211.
86. See footnote 48.
87. *Iphigenia in Tauris*, 577-583.

and necklaces. Second are those arising from reasoning.

17. In constructing plots and working them out
in diction the poet ought to place the action before his eyes as much as possible. For in this way,
seeing everything most distinctly just as though
25   what is done had arisen in front of him, he will
discover what is fitting and will least forget incongruities. A sign of this is the censure given to Karkinos, for the return of Amphiaros from the tem-
ple would have been overlooked by the spectators
had it not been seen, but on the stage it failed because the incongruity annoyed them.
30   As far as possible he ought even to work out the
incidents in gestures, for apart from nature itself
those are most persuasive who themselves suffer the
passions they are imitating. He who is himself dis-
tressed most truly distresses, and he who is angry
most truly enrages. On this account poetic science
belongs to those either naturally well-endowed or
mad, for of these the former mould themselves well
[to the passion required], the latter are entranced.
The arguments [of the plots], both those already
1455ᵇ   made-up and those produced by the poet himself,
ought to be set forth universally and then extended by introducing episodes.⁸⁸ What is universal in the *Iphigenia,* for example, might be contemplated in this way: a certain maiden, having
been sacrificed, disappears mysteriously from those
5   who sacrificed her and is settled in another land
in which it is the custom to sacrifice strangers to
the goddess, and this priesthood she holds. At a
later time the brother of the priestess happens to
come there. That a god appointed him to go there

88. For a discussion of the argument of plots see p. 116.

for a cause is external to the universal [argument].[89] That for which he came is external to the plot.[90] He comes and is seized, and as he is about to be sacrificed he is recognized, either as
10 Euripides made the recognition or as Polyidos made it, when he mentions with likelihood that not only his sister, but also he himself is to be sacrificed, and thereupon he is saved.

After this, having assumed names [for the agents], the episodes are introduced. And one ✓ must be sure the episodes are appropriate, as are the madness of Orestes because of which he was
15 seized [91] and his being saved through purification.[92] Yet while in dramas the episodes are cut short, in epic-making they are lengthened. For the argument of the *Odyssey* is not long. A certain man has been abroad for many years, is closely watched by Poseidon, and is all alone. Moreover,
20 his affairs at home are such that his wealth is being squandered by suitors to his wife and schemes are being laid against his son. Tempest-tossed, he arrives; there is a recognition, and he sets upon his enemies, saving himself and destroying them. This, then, is what is proper [to the argument]; the rest is episode.

18. In every tragedy there is both involvement
25 and solution. The involvement includes whatever

89. I.e. Apollo's reason for wanting Orestes to bring the statue of Artemis to Athens is neither acted (which would make it part of the plot) nor narrated (which would make it part of the argument).
90. I.e. that Orestes is to bring back the statue of Artemis to Athens is narrated by Orestes (85-90 and 976-979) and Athena (1438-1441). It is the narration and not the incident narrated that is part of the plot.
91. This is narrated by the herdsman, 238-339.
92. This is foretold by Athena, 1438-1455.

is external [to the plot] [93] and often some of the
internal incidents. What remains is solution. By
the involvement I mean that part of the tragedy
from the beginning to that part ultimately from
which the agent changes to good fortune [or mis-
fortune], and by solution I mean that part from
the beginning of the change to the end. Thus in
30 the *Lynkeus* by Theodektes the involvement includes both the previous incidents and the seizure
of the child as well as the seizure of those who
seized him, while the solution is that part from
the indictment for the death to the end.

There are four forms of tragedy, for the parts
we spoke of are this many.[94] [1] The complex
tragedy of which the whole is reversal and recognition. [2] The tragedy of suffering, e.g. the vari-
1456ᵃ ous *Ajaxes*[95] and *Ixions*. [3] The tragedy of character, e.g. *The Phthian Women* and the *Peleus*.
[4] The fourth is [the tragedy of spectacle],[96] e.g.
The Daughters of Phorcys and the *Prometheus*,[97]
as well as those taking place in Hades. Now above
all, poets ought to try to have all these forms in
their tragedies, but if they cannot, then the great-
5 est of them and most of them. Otherwise men will
carp at them as they do now. For while there have
come to be good poets in respect of each part of
tragedy, men expect one poet to surpass each of
the goods proper to other poets. Rather it is just
to speak of tragedies as being the same or different
in respect of plot above all else, those being the

93. Yet still part of the argument. An incident external to
the plot is also said to be external to the drama. Cf. 1453ᵇ 32
and 1454ᵇ 3.
94. For an explanation of these four forms of tragedy see
pp. 118–21.
95. The *Ajax* of Sophokles is one that survives.
96. The text is corrupt at this point. I have followed Bywater's emendation for reasons that appear in the analysis.
97. By Aeschylos.

same which have the same complication and solution.[98] Many poets complicate their tragedies well
10   but solve them badly,[99] yet both ought always to
be mastered.

One ought also to remember, as we have often
mentioned, not to produce a tragedy with an epic-
making construction. By epic-making I mean a
many [actioned] plot, as there would be if one
were to make a tragedy from the whole plot of
the *Iliad*. For in the epic, because of its length,
the parts take on a fitting magnitude, but in
15   dramas many actions result in a departure from
the conception of tragedy. A sign of this is that
those who have made tragedies of the whole of
the sack of Ilion and not part by part as did Euripides, or of the whole of what happened to Niobe,
and not a part of this as did Aeschylos, either fail
or do badly in the contests, since even Agathon
failed only in this respect. Yet in their reversals
20   and simple incidents these poets are wondrously
able to hit upon what they wish, for what they
wish is the tragic and the humane. This is produced whenever the wise but villainous man, such
as Sisyphos, is deceived, or the courageous but unjust man is worsted. And this, as Agathon says, is
likely, for it is likely that many incidents will
25   arise against likelihood.

And the chorus ought to be conceived as one
of the performers, as part of the whole and as
sharing in the contest, not as in the tragedies of

98. Therefore, it is unjust to compare two kinds of plot,
e.g. one of character with one of recognition, for each kind
can be perfect in its kind. In fact, if one attempted to make
a plot of character complex, the solution would be episodic,
since it would not be pertinent to the argument.
99. To censure a drama because of a disparity between involvement and solution, however, is just, for the drama is
then being censured by criteria which the drama itself assumes in its argument.

Euripides, but as in those of Sophokles. In the remaining poets the parts that are sung no more
belong to the plot than they do to any other tragedy. On this account they sing interludes of the
30   sort that Agathon first began. And yet what difference is there between singing interludes and adapt-
ing an expression or a whole episode from one
drama to another?

19. Since the other parts have already been
mentioned, it remains to speak about diction and
35   thought. Let us assume what has been said about
thought in the *Rhetoric,* for thought is more
proper to that method. Whatever there may be
in tragedy by virtue of thought, these are the
things that ought to be rendered through speech.
The parts of this are demonstrating, solving, and
1456ᵇ   rendering the passions (e.g. pity, fear, anger, and
such), and moreover, maximizing and minimizing
things. It is evident that the poet ought to use the
same forms in the incidents as well, whenever he
ought to render the piteous, the terrible, the maxi-
5   mal, or the likely, except for this difference, that
the forms of the incidents ought to be apparent
without explanation, while those of the speeches
ought to be rendered by the speaker in the speech
and ought to arise with the speech. For what
would the function of a speaker be if things appeared as they ought and yet not through the
speech?

Of things concerning diction one form of theory
10   is of the [inflectional] modes of diction, the knowledge of which belongs to the art of declamation
and the man who possesses such an architectonic
art. It says, for example, what an injunction is, a
prayer, a description, a threat, a question, an answer, or anything else of this sort. For the knowledge or ignorance of these brings to poetic science

15 no censure deserving of the effort. For who could conceive of any mistake in Homer's "Sing, Goddess, of the wrath . . ." [100] which Protagoras censures because when he speaks Homer commands where he is supposed to pray. For to order something done or not done, he says, is to give a command. On this account we may pass over this subject of theory as belonging to another art and not to poetic science.

20   20. All diction has the following parts: the element [or the letter], the syllable, the conjunction, the joint, the noun, the verb, the case, and the speech.

The element is indivisible voice, yet not all voice, but only that from which comprehensible voice naturally arises. For beasts also utter indivisible voices, none of which I call an element of dic-

25 tion. The parts of indivisible voice are the vocal, the semi-vocal, and the non-vocal. The vocal is that which has audible voice without the application [of the tongue or lip], the semi-vocal is that which has audible voice with the application [of the tongue or lip], e.g. S and R, while the non-vocal is that which has no voice in itself even with the application [of the tongue or lip] but which

30 becomes audible when accompanied by elements possessing voice, e.g. G and D. The elements differ in respect of the shape of the mouth and their place within the mouth, in roughness and smoothness, in length and shortness, and moreover, in being acute, grave, or intermediate. The particulars concerning these things are the business of the theory of metrics.

35 The syllable is non-significant voice synthesized from non-vocal and vocal elements, for both GR

100. The opening line of the *Iliad*.

without A and GR with A, as in GRA, are syllables. But the theory concerning these differences also belongs to metrics.

The conjunction is non-significant voice which 1457ᵃ neither prevents nor produces the natural synthesis of one significant voice from many voices, and which is not by virtue of itself suitably placed at the beginning of speech, e.g. μέν, δή, τοί, δέ. Or else it is non-significant voice which naturally pro-
5 duces one significant voice from many individual
7 significant voices, e.g. ἀμφί, περί, and others.

6 A joint is non-significant voice which makes evident the beginning, end, or division of speech, and
10 is naturally placed both at the extremes and at the middle of the speech.[101]

A noun is synthesized significant voice that does not indicate time and of which no part is significant by virtue of itself. For in doubled nouns we do not use the parts as being significant by virtue of themselves: e.g. in Θεοδώρος (Theodore) the δῶρον is not significant [as a part].

A verb is synthesized significant voice that does
15 indicate time and of which no part, as in the case of nouns, is significant by virtue of itself. For "man" and "white" do not signify when, but "walks" and "has walked" signify in addition present and past time.

The case of either nouns or verbs is that which
20 signifies the relations "of," "to," and such; or whether something is one or many, e.g. "man" and "men"; or matters of declamation, e.g. question or command, for "walked?" and "walk!" are cases of the verb "to walk" by virtue of these forms.

Speech is synthesized significant voice of which some parts by virtue of themselves signify some-

101. The text is corrupt from 1457ᵃ 2-9. I have followed Bywater's emendation.

25 thing, for not all speech is composed of verbs
and nouns, e.g. the definition of man, for there
may be speech without verbs. Yet some part always
has significance in itself, e.g. "Kleon" in "the
walking Kleon." Speech is unified in two ways,
for it is one either by signifying one thing or by
the conjunction of many parts. The *Iliad,* for ex-
30 ample, is one by conjunction, while the definition
of man is one by signifying one thing.102

21. The form of a word may be single, by which
I mean that which is not composed of significant
parts, e.g. "earth," or double, i.e. that which is
composed either of both significant and non-significant parts (except that they are not significant
or non-significant within the word103) or of parts
that are all significant. There may also be triple,
35 quadruple, or many-fold words, e.g. many amplified words such as "Hermokaikoxanthos."
1457ᵇ Every word is either authoritative, foreign, metaphorical, ornamental, made-up, extended, contracted, or altered. By authoritative I mean one
used by everyone, by foreign one that is used by
others. It is apparent that it is possible for the
5 same word to be both authoritative and foreign,
but not to the same people, for σίγυνον (spear)104
is authoritative to the Cyprians, but foreign to us.
A metaphor is the transfer of a word belonging
to something else, a transference either from genus
to species, from species to genus, from species to
species, or according to an analogy. [1] By genus
10 to species I mean, e.g. "There stands my ship," 105
for "being anchored" is a species of "standing."
[2] From species to genus is, e.g. "Verily, ten

102. For a discussion of this point see p. 127.
103. Cf. 1457ᵃ 12.
104. To Athenians the authoritative word for spear would
be σιγύνης.
105. *Odyssey,* I, 185 and XXIV, 308.

thousand kind deeds has Odysseus done," [106] for "ten thousand" is a species of "many" and is here used instead of it. [3] From species to species is, e.g. "Drawing off his soul with a blade of bronze" and "Cutting [the blood] with a stout bronze

15 bowl," [107] for here "drawing off" is used for "cutting" and "cutting" for "drawing off," since both are species of "removing." [4] There is an analogy whenever there are four terms such that the relation between the second and the first is similar to that between the fourth and the third. For instead of the second the poet expresses the fourth, and instead of the fourth the second. And some-

20 times poets add to the metaphor the relative of the word supplanted. I mean, e.g. since a cup is to Dionysos as a shield is to Ares, the poet will call the cup "the shield of Dionysos" or the shield "the cup of Ares." Or again, since old age is to life as evening is to day, he will call evening "the old age of day" or what Empedokles called it, and old age

25 he will call "the evening of life" or "the sunset of life." In some cases the word assumed in the analogy does not exist, yet nonetheless the metaphor can be stated in the same way. For example, to scatter seed is to sow, but that which concerns the flame of the sun is nameless. But since this is to the sun as sowing is to the seed, the poet will say

30 "sowing the God-created flame." Besides this manner of using metaphor one may call something by a word belonging to something else and deny of it something appropriate to that word, e.g. calling the shield, not "the cup of Ares," but "the cup without wine."

A word which is made-up is one not generally used by anyone, but put down by the poet him-

35 self, for some of them seem to be of this sort, e.g.

106. *Iliad*, II, 272.
107. See below, footnote 110.

"sprouters" for horns and "prayerer" for priest.
1458ᵃ A word is extended when a longer vocal element
is used than what is appropriate to it, or when
a syllable is inserted, e.g. πόληος for πόλεως and
Πηληιάδεω for Πηλείδου. A word is contracted when
5 some part of it is removed, e.g. κρῖ [for κριθή], δῶ
[for δῶμα], and μία γίνεται ἀμφοτέρων ὄψ.¹⁰⁸ A word
is altered when part of it remains and part is
made-up, e.g. δεξιτερὸν κατὰ μαζόν instead of δεξιόν.¹⁰⁹
Nouns themselves are masculine, feminine, or
neuter. Those nouns are masculine which end in
10 ν, ρ, and s, or in elements composed of this last
letter, these being two, ψ and ξ. Those nouns are
feminine which end in vocal elements which are
always long, as η and ω, and in α among extend-
ible elements. Thus there happen to be an equal
number of endings for masculine and feminine,
for ψ and ξ are the same in ending as s. No noun
15 ends in a non-vocal or in a short vocal. There are
only three that end in ι; μέλι, κόμμι, and πέπερι.
Five end in υ. Neuter nouns end in these elements
and in ν and s.

22. The virtue of diction is to be clear and not
abject. Diction arising from authoritative words
20 is clearest, yet abject. Examples of this would be
the making of Kleophon and Sthenelos. On the
other hand, diction that uses strange words is dignified and alters what is idiomatic. By strange
words I mean foreign words, metaphors, extensions, and all besides authoritative words. But if
one were to produce diction entirely from words
of this sort, the diction would be either an enigma

108. The text is corrupt at this point. Instead of ὄψ it reads
όησ as it read όησ at 1456ᵃ 2. The ὄψ would be a contraction
of ὄψις, spectacle.
109. *Iliad*, V, 393.

25   or a barbarism: an enigma if produced from metaphors, a barbarism if produced from foreign words.
For the form of an enigma is this, the combina-
tion in speech of attributes impossible of being
connected. This may be produced with a synthesis
of metaphors, but not with [authoritative] words,
30   e.g. "I saw a man welding bronze to a man with
fire," 110 and such. A barbarism arises from foreign
words.

These forms of words ought, therefore, to be
blended in some way, for what is not idiomatic
produces diction which is not abject, e.g. the
foreign word, the metaphor, the ornamental word,
and the other forms mentioned, while the authoritative produces clearness. Not the least part
1458ᵇ   of bringing together clarity of diction and the
non-idiomatic is the use of the extension, shorten-
ing, and alteration of words. For because they are
different from the authoritative, since they arise
counter to what is customary, they produce what
is not idiomatic, and yet because they share some-
5   thing with the customary they have clarity.

Thus they do not rightly find fault who censure
this manner of discourse and ridicule the poets as
did Eukleides the elder. He said it was easy to
make poems if permitted to lengthen words as
much as one wishes,111 and he made a lampoon in

110. The answer to the riddle or enigma is the cupping-
bowl, also mentioned at 1457ᵇ 14. This was a bronze vessel
used for drawing blood. Heated lint was placed in the vessel
and its mouth was applied to a small incision. The resulting
reduction of pressure caused a strong flow of blood.

111. In Greek poetry the meter depends upon differences
in the length of the vowels rather than on differences in the
stress of syllables as in English. If a short vowel falls where a
long one is demanded by the meter the effect is an unnatural
lengthening of that vowel which becomes ridiculous if employed without taste. A parallel to this in English poetry
would be the excessive stressing of normally unaccented syllables in order to satisfy the meter. Cf. 1458ᵃ 1.

this very diction. " Ἐπιχάρην εἶδον Μαραθῶνάδε
10 βαδίζοντα" and "οὐκ ἄν γ' ἐράμενος τὸν ἐκείνου
ἐλλέβορον." Still, it is certainly ludicrous to use
the extension of words in such a manner as to
make it in any way apparent. Indeed, moderation
belongs to all parts of diction in common. For the
same thing can be executed with metaphors, foreign words, and other forms if they are used un-
15 fittingly and purposely to produce the ludicrous.
How great a difference it makes to use words
suitably can be observed in epics when authoritative words are set in the place of others in the
meter. Replace any foreign word, metaphor, or
other of these forms with some authoritative word
and you will see the truth of what we say. For
20 example, Aeschylos and Euripides made the same
iambic with only one word replaced, a foreign
word instead of the customary and authoritative,
but the one is beautiful, the other trivial. For
Aeschylos in the *Philoktetes* makes the iamb "A
cancer eats away the flesh of this my foot," while
Euripides replaces "eats away" with "feasts upon."
25 And the same thing can be seen if the words
"Being now that I am slight and worthless and
unseemly," [112] were replaced by these authoritative words, "Being now that I am small and weak
and ugly," and if "Having set an unseemly chair
and a meager table," [113] were replaced by "Hav-
30 ing set a weak chair and a small table," or "The
sea-shore roars" [114] by "The sea-shore sounds."
Moreover, Ariphrades ridiculed the tragedians for
using words which no one would express in discourse, e.g. "from the house away" instead of
"away from the house," and "thou," and "ἐγὼ δέ
1459ª νιν," and "Achilleus near" instead of "near Achil-

112. *Odyssey*, IX, 515.
113. *Ibid.*, II, 259.
114. *Iliad*, XVII, 265.

leus," and others of this sort. For because they are not made with authoritative words all such words make the diction non-idiomatic, and of this he was ignorant.

5 It is a great thing to make a fitting use of each of the forms mentioned as well as double and foreign words, but greatest is the use of metaphors. For this alone cannot be gained from others and is a sign of the naturally well-endowed poet, for to make good metaphors is to observe similarities among dissimilarities. Among words, doubles are

10 most suitable for dithyrambs, foreign words for heroic[115] poems, and metaphors for iambics.[116] Indeed, in heroic poems all the forms mentioned are useful, while in iambics, because it is mostly diction that is imitated, those words are suitable which one might use in speech, these being such words as the authoritative, the metaphor, and the ornamental.

15 Concerning tragedy, therefore, and imitation through acting, what has been expressed is adequate.

23. Of that which is descriptive and imitates in meter,[117] it is evident that the plot, as in tragedy, ought to be constructed dramatically[118] and be of a single action which is whole and complete and

20 which has a beginning, middle, and end, in order that it produce, like a single, whole animal, its appropriate pleasure. And it ought not to put down anything similar to our customary histories, in which, of necessity, it is not a single action which is made evident, but a single time and what-

115. See footnote 31.
116. Tragedy and comedy are among those poetic forms written in iambic. Cf. 1449ᵃ 23.
117. I.e. epic.
118. See footnote 23.

ever happens in that time, to one character or
many, each incident being related to the others
25 as it happened. For just as the sea-fight at Salamis
and the battle with the Carthaginians in Sicily
arose at the same time, yet were not exerted to
the same end, so also in a succession of time some
incidents arise after others with no one end arising. Yet this is what most poets do in their poems.
30 On this account, as we have already mentioned,[119]
in comparison with the others Homer appears
divinely inspired in not attempting to make a
poem of the whole war, though indeed, it had a
beginning and an end. For it would have been
too great and not easily seen together, or if mod-
erated in respect of magnitude, it would have been
too complicated in the variety of its incidents. As
35 it is, while taking only one part of the war, he
uses many episodes from other parts, e.g. the
catalogue of ships[120] and other episodes, to diver-
sify his making. The others make their epics about
1459ᵇ one man, or one time, or an action which, though
one, has many parts, e.g. those who made *The
Cypria* and *The Little Iliad.* Accordingly, only
one or two tragedies are to be made from either
the *Iliad* or the *Odyssey,* while many are to be
5 made from *The Cypria;* and from *The Little Iliad*
there have been more than eight: *The Judgment
of Arms, Philoktetes, Neoptolemos, Eurypylos,
The Begging, The Laconian Women, The Sack of
Ilion,* and *The Departure of the Fleet,* as well as
Sinon and *The Trojan Women.*

Moreover,[121] epic-making ought to have the
same forms as those of tragedy (for it will be either

119. 1451ᵃ 22.
120. *Iliad,* II, 484-760.
121. Traditionally chapter 24 has begun at this point rather
than at 1459ᵇ 17. This paragraph, however, by its subject
matter belongs in chapter 23. See p. 134.

simple, complex, of character, or of suffering) as
10   well as the same [formal] parts (excluding the
making of melody and spectacle). For epics also
ought to have reversals, recognitions, and sufferings. Moreover, thought and diction ought to be
beautifully made in epics also. All of these were
first and adequately used by Homer, for of his
poems the construction of the *Iliad* is simple and
15   of suffering, while that of the *Odyssey* is complex
(since there is recognition through the whole of
it) and of character,[122] and in addition to this he
surpasses all others in diction and thought.

24. Epic-making differs from tragedy in the
length of its construction and in its meter. Now
what we have already mentioned is an adequate
limit to length,[123] for it ought to be possible to
20   see the beginning and the end together. This will
be so if the constructions of epics have less length
than those of the ancients yet are as long as the
number of tragedies put alongside one another at
one hearing. In regard to extending its magnitude
there is a great advantage which is proper to epic-
making, because in tragedy one may not imitate
25   many parts being done at the same time, but only
that part which is on the stage and belongs to the
performers, while in epic-making, because it is descriptive, one may make many parts achieved at
once, and these, if appropriate, increase the mass
of the poem. With a view to magnificence, chang-
30   ing [the attention of] the hearer, and introducing
dissimilar episodes this is a good, for it is the sameness of the incidents which, by quickly satisfying
the hearer, makes tragedies fail.

122. For an explanation of this double classification in the
case of epic see p. 135.
123. 1450^b 34-1451^a 15.

Trial has shown that for epic the suitable meter is the heroic. For if one were to produce a descriptive imitation in any other meter, or in many meters, the lack of fitness would be apparent. For 35 the heroic is the most stately and massive of meters, and on this account it admits of foreign names and metaphors more than any other, for descriptive imitation is extravagant in comparison with others. Iambic and tetrameter, on the other hand, 1460ᵃ are meters of motion, the latter involved in dancing, the former in acting. Moreover, it would be even more absurd if one were to mix meters as did Chairemon. On this account no one has produced a long poetic construction in any other meter than the heroic. Rather, as we expressed above,[124] nature itself teaches us the suitable meter 5 to pick.

But Homer, while deserving praise for many other things, is deserving also because of all poets he alone is not ignorant of what he ought to produce of himself in the poem. For the poet himself ought to speak the least of all, since he is not an imitator by virtue of this.[125] While other poets engage in the contest themselves throughout the whole poem and imitate but little and seldom, 10 Homer, after making a short preface, at once brings in a man, woman, or other character, none of them characterless, but each possessing his own character.

Now while the poet ought to produce the wondrous in tragedy, the unreasonable (through which the wondrous most often happens) may be produced more easily in epic-making because what is done is not seen. For the incidents concerning

124. 1449ᵃ 24.
125. For an explanation of this statement see p. 136. and cf. *Iliad,* I, 1-7 and II, 484-492.

15　the pursuit of Hektor would appear ludicrous on
the stage with the Greeks standing still and not
pursuing and Achilleus waving them back,[126] but
in epics this is overlooked. And the wondrous is
pleasant. A sign of this is that all men add to their
narratives by way of being agreeable. And it has
been Homer most of all who has taught the others
20　how one ought to use falsehoods. This is by means
of misreasoning. For whenever, if one thing exists
or comes to be, a later thing exists or comes to
be, men suppose that, if the later exists or comes
to be, then the earlier exists. But this is false. On
this account, if the first be false, but of necessity
a later thing exists or comes to be if the first
exists, one ought only to add that the later exists.
25　For because it knows the later to be true, our soul
misreasons that the first exists. An example of this
occurs in the washing of Odysseus.[127] Not only
ought the poet to choose impossible likelihoods
rather than unpersuasive possibilities, but he ought
not to construct arguments from unreasonable
parts. Rather there should, in the main, be nothing unreasonable, but if there is, then it ought to
30　be external to what has been plotted, as is Oedipus'
not knowing how Laios was killed, and not in the
drama, as is the narration of the Pythian games
in the *Elektra*[128] or the voiceless man coming from
Tegea to Mysia in *The Mysians*. Thus to say that
the plot would be ruined is ludicrous, for from

126. *Iliad*, XXII, 205.
127. *Odyssey*, XIX, 164-260. Odysseus, disguised as a Cretan,
convinces his wife Penelope that he has seen her husband.
She assumes that if he has seen Odysseus he can describe him.
When he successfully describes Odysseus she falsely reasons
that he has seen him.
128. By Sophokles, 680-763. Aristotle may be supposing that
it is unreasonable that Elektra and Klytaimnestra should not
have heard of the results of the Pythian games and therefore
'nown that the tale of the paidagogos was false.

the beginning one should not construct a plot of
this sort, and if such a plot be put down and it
35 appears that it might be made more reasonably,
then it is absurd as well as unreasonable. For it is
evident that even the unreasonable incidents in
the *Odyssey* about his putting to shore[129] would
1460ᵇ have become intolerable if produced by a base
poet. As it is, the poet veils what is absurd by
using other goods to make the incidents pleasing.
Yet the diction ought to be elaborated in the func-
tionless parts, i.e. the parts which involve neither
character nor thought, for diction that is over-
5 brilliant merely obscures characters and thought.

25. Let us now consider problems and their solutions. How many forms of them there are, and
of what sort, will become apparent if we contem-
plate them in the following way. Since the poet is
an imitator, just as the painter from life or any
other maker of likenesses, of necessity [A] he al-
10 ways imitates one of three things: either such as
were or are, such as are said or seem to be, or such
as ought to be. These are reported in [B] diction
or in foreign words and metaphors. And there are
many modifications of diction, for modifications
are permitted to poets. In addition to this, rightness in politics and in poetic science are not the
15 same, nor are they in poetic science and any other
art. And concerning poetic science itself there are
two sorts of mistakes, one which is essential, the
other accidental. For if the poet has chosen to imitate but has·an inability to do so, then the mistake
is essential to poetic science. But if, in choosing to
imitate incorrectly (e.g. a horse throwing both right
legs forward), he makes a mistake in some art (e.g.

129. XIII, 116ff. While Odysseus is sleeping his men move
him and his goods from the ship to the shore without awaken-
ing him.

20 that of medicine or any other art) or produces an impossibility of any sort, then the mistake is not essential to poetic science. We ought to conduct our examination from these premises, then, in finding solutions to censures involving poetic problems.

[A] Let us first concern ourselves with those problems relating to art itself. If the poet has produced an impossibility, then he has made a mistake, but [1] rightly so, if this happens to serve the
25 end of poetic science (for this end has been mentioned 130) and thus makes this or any other part more astounding. An example of this is the pursuit of Hektor. However, if this end may be attributed more so, or even no less, while still being in accord with the art concerned with that mistake, then the mistake is not rightly made, for in general, if it may be so, there ought to be no mistakes. Moreover, [2] [it is important to determine] whether the
30 mistake is one according to art or accidental and according to something else. For it is less of a mistake not to know that a female deer has no horns than to paint unimitatively.131 In addition to this, a poem may be censured because it is not true. But perhaps [3] what is imitated is what ought to be, and it is by this that the problem is to be solved. For example, Sophokles said that he himself made men such as they ought to be while
35 Euripides made them such as they are. And if neither of these is the case, then perhaps [4] what

130. The "end" of a work of art is its function conceived as an internal principle of organization. The end mentioned was the catharsis of pity and fear, the function of both epic and tragedy. Cf. 1449^b 27, 1453^b 10-14, and 1462^b 13.

131. To imitate is to give unity of form to materials according to an internal functional principle. To paint unimitatively would therefore be to fail to achieve such unity in the painting.

is imitated is such as men say, e.g. what men say about the gods. For perhaps what they say about the gods happens to be as Xenophanes said, nei-
1461ᵃ ther the better thing to say nor true, yet still it is what men say. In other cases perhaps what is imitated is not the better thing but rather [5] what is the case [or what is true], e.g. what was expressed concerning the arms: "Their spears stood upright with their butt-spikes in the ground." [132] For this was the custom then as it is now in Illyria. As to
5 whether something is expressed or done nobly or not, we must consider [6] not only what is expressed or done in itself to see if it is worthy or base, but also who did or said it, to whom, when, by what means, and for the sake of what, e.g. to bring about a greater good or ward off a greater evil.

10 [B] Some problems ought to be solved by looking to the diction, e.g. the poet may have used [7] a foreign word, as in "οὐρῆας μὲν πρῶτον," [133] for perhaps he speaks of guards and not mules,[134] and when he says of Dolon "He was indeed of evil form," [135] perhaps it is not that his body was deformed but that his face was ugly, for the Cretans call the fair-faced the well-formed. Again, "Mix it
15 livelier" [136] may mean, not undiluted as for drunkards, but more quickly.[137] Other things [8] may be expressed according to a metaphor, e.g. "The other gods and men slept all the night" [138] is said to-

132. *Iliad*, X, 152.
133. *Ibid.*, I, 50.
134. οὐρεύς might mean οὖρος, guard, rather than ὀρεύς mule.
135. *Iliad*, X, 316.
136. *Ibid.*, IX, 202.
137. The ancient Greeks customarily diluted their wine with water in varying ratios.
138. *Iliad*, II, 1, with which compare X, 1.

gether with "Indeed, on gazing at the Trojan
plain, he marvelled at the din of flutes and
pipes," [139] for "all" is expressed rather than
20 "much" according to a metaphor since it is a
species of "much." And "She alone has no part" [140]
is expressed according to a metaphor, for the one
who is most known stands alone. Some problems
are to be solved [9] by changing the intonation, as
in the solutions of Hippias of Thasos: "δίδομεν δέ
οἱ" [141] and "τὸ μὲν οὗ καταπύθεται ὄμβρω." [142] Some
are solved [10] by dividing the words, as in these
lines by Empedokles, "Suddenly things became
25 mortal which before had learned to be immortal,
and pure before mixed." [143] Some are solved [11]
by noting an ambiguity, as in "Full two parts of
the night is spent," for here πλείω is ambiguous.[144]
Some are solved [12] by showing the words to be
in accordance with the custom in diction, e.g.
since the blending of wine and water is said to
be wine, the poet makes the words "greaves of
new-wrought tin," [145] or since those working in
30 iron are called braziers, the poet mentions that
Ganymedes pours wine for Zeus, although the gods
do not drink wine.[146] The latter, however, might
be a metaphor.

139. *Ibid.*, X, 11.
140. *Ibid.*, XVIII, 489.
141. Instead of δίδομεν, *ibid.*, II, 15, changing a false statement to an unfulfilled command.
142. Instead of οὐ, *ibid.*, XXIII, 327, changing a false nega-
tive to a true affirmative.
143. I.e., does the break come before or after the word "before"; either something became pure which was before mixed,
or was pure before and became mixed. The latter is no doubt
Empedokles' intention.
144. *Iliad*, X, 252. It may mean either "full" or "more
than."
145. *Ibid.*, XXI, 592. Greaves were a "blend" of tin and
copper.
146. *Ibid.*, XX, 234.

Whenever a word seems to signify an incongruity one ought to examine the number of ways it might be significant in what has been expressed. For example, in "there the bronze spear was stopped" [147] one ought to examine the number of ways in which a spear might be hindered. One ought to

35   examine the word in this way and that way, so as
1461ᵇ to conceive of it in a way most opposite to that of which Glaukon speaks. For he says that some men unreasonably preconceive [the significance of a poet's words] and [from these preconceptions] reason to conclusions which they themselves condemn. Then they censure what it seems to them the poet has expressed if it is incongruous with their own suppositions. This is how the incidents concerning Ikarios have suffered. For they suppose

5   him to be a Lakonian and therefore find it absurd that Telemachos did not happen to meet him when he went to Lakedaimon. Yet perhaps it is as the Kephallenians say, that Odysseus married one of their people and that her father was Ikadios, not Ikarios, so that it is likely that the problem exists because of a mistake.

In general, the poet ought to bring in the im-
10   possible with regard to the making itself, or what is better, or common opinion. For with regard to the making, a persuasive impossibility is to be picked over an unpersuasive possibility, and if it is impossible that there be such men as Zeuxis paints, still they are better than what men are, for the poem ought to surpass the example. He ought to bring in the unreasonable with regard to what

15   men say and also because at times it is not unreasonable, for what is against likelihood is also likely to arise. What is expressed incongruously ought to be considered, as are refutations in argu-

147. *Ibid.*, XX, 272.

ments, to see whether one is speaking of the same thing, in relation to the same thing, and in the same way, so that one says either the same thing or something related to what one has said, or else what a prudent man would assume. Censure of unreasonableness and wickedness is right whenever 20 there is no necessity and no use is made of the unreasonableness, as in the action of Aigeus in Euripides' *Medea*,[148] or of the villainy, as in the action of Menelaos in the *Orestes*.[149]

Censures, therefore, are brought forth from five species, for a thing may be censured as being impossible, unreasonable, noxious, incongruous, or against rightness according with some art. The so- 25 lutions will take into consideration the things we have mentioned, these being twelve in number.[150]

26. One might raise the question whether the epic-making or the tragic imitation is better. For if the better is the less vulgar, and this is always what is relative to better spectators, it is evident that what imitates relative to all men is vulgar. For performers suppose that the spectators do not 30 perceive what is imitated if they do not add something of their own, and so they make many motions, as base aulos players roll about when imitating the discus and maul the leader of the chorus when playing the aulos in the *Skylla*. Now it is said that tragedy is of this sort, as the earlier performers supposed the later ones to be, for Myn- 35 niskos used to call Kallippides "the ape" because he overacted, and the same sort of opinion was 1462ª held of Pindaros. The whole art of tragedy, then, is said to be to epic-making as the later performers

148. *Medea*, 663.
149. *Orestes*, 682-716.
150. The twelve solutions to censures have been numbered in the translation.

are to the earlier, and epic-making is said to be
relative to equitable spectators having no need of
gestures, while tragedy is relative to the base. And
if tragedy is vulgar, it is evident that it is worse.

5   Now first of all, this accusation is not made of
poetic science, but of the art of declamation, since
one may overwork visual signs even when recit-
ing,[151] as did Sosistratos, or when singing, as did
Mnasitheos the Opuntian. Then too, one must not
reject all motion if indeed dancing is not to be
rejected, but rather that of base performers. This
10   was the censure made of Kallippides, and nowadays of others, for imitating illiberal women.
Moreover, the end of tragedy is produced without the motions of performers just as is the end
of epic-making, for it is apparent of what sort a
tragedy is merely through the reading of it. Therefore, if in other respects tragedy is better, the at-
tribution of baseness is at least not necessary.

In the second place, [1] tragedy has all the parts
15   that epic-making has, for it is admissible even to
use epic meter. And moreover, music and spectacles, through which the pleasures of tragedy are
most distinctly constructed, are not parts of little
importance. Then too, this distinctness exists both
in the reading of tragedy and in these functions.
Moreover, [2] the end of the imitation is achieved
1462[b] in less length, for what is concentrated is more
pleasant than what is diluted through greater
time, as would be seen if one were to put the
Oedipus by Sophokles into an epic as long as the
Iliad. Moreover, [3] the imitation of epic poets
has less unity, a sign of this being that from any
5   kind of epic imitation many tragedies arise, so
that if the poet produces an epic plot which is
unified it appears either curtailed if shown briefly,

151. I.e. even in the recitation of narrative works like epic.

or watery if it follows the epic measure of length.
In saying that epics are composed of many actions
I mean, for example, that the *Iliad* and the *Odyssey* have many parts of this sort which have magni-
10 tude by virtue of themselves. And yet these poems
are constructed as well as they may be and each
is, as much as may be, an imitation of one action.
Therefore, if tragedy differs in all these respects,
and moreover, [4] in respect of the function of
art (for these two ought to produce, not any pleasure that might happen, but rather what has been
expressed [152]), it is apparent that it is better, since
15 it happens to achieve its end more completely
than does epic-making.

Concerning tragedy and epic-making, therefore,
the forms and the parts of these, in how many and
in what respects they differ, some of the causes of
their being well made or not, as well as censures
and their solutions, let what we have expressed
suffice.

152. 1449[b] 27 and *passim.*

ARISTOTLE'S POETICS

ANALYSIS

ANALYSIS

I. *Aristotle's General Conception of the Problems of Art*

According to Aristotle's general conception of science the inquiry into problems concerning works of art constitutes a science. For there is a science whenever there exists a subject matter whose attributes can be examined in order to gain warranted conclusions concerning the intrinsic nature of that subject. The possibility of a science concerned with art therefore rests on the same ultimate basis as the possibility of a science concerned with nature. For in either case there is an object to be examined, and it is the experienced properties of this object which test the adequacy of statements made about that object. The science of art (or productive science, as Aristotle called it) depends, then, upon the consideration of the art work as an object which has in itself certain characteristics apart from its relations to other things. For however the art work might come into existence and whatever effects or consequences it might have on those who view it, nonetheless just because it is a thing it must have a nature of its own.

The supposition that art either can or ought to be examined independently of other parts of man's experience was hotly contested in Aristotle's day and is still the subject of polemical debate today. Most treatises concerned with art, in fact, do not deal with its intrinsic characteristics. That is, they do not deal with the art object as such. Instead we find essays on art as the expression of various biological, sociological, political, or psychological forces operating on the artist. Or we find discussions on art as an instrument for the moral im-

59

provement of man, or art as a technique for eliciting various emotional responses in an audience. Aristotle's position does not imply that such discussions on art are meaningless or impossible. There are in fact countless references throughout his works to the relationships which can be found between art and other things which form a part of man's world. But these discussions have other purposes than that of telling us what art is or what makes a poem, painting, or musical composition well or poorly made. They might tell us what kind of art is most suitable for the moral improvement of man (as does the discussion of music in Aristotle's *Politics*), or they might indicate how art can be used for the purpose of effecting a given response in an audience (as does the discussion of literary devices in his *Rhetoric*). But none of these inquiries is concerned with the *nature* of a work of art—that is, what it is in itself as a self-subsisting thing—and therefore they form no part of productive science.

It is Aristotle's general philosophic method which leads him to distinguish between the intrinsic properties of art works and those attributes which they possess only in relation to other things. In general, Aristotle's procedure involves a distinction between three kinds of science which he calls the theoretical, the practical, and the productive. Each deals with a different kind of problem. Theoretical science is concerned with problems of knowing. Practical science is concerned with problems of doing, i.e. problems of action. Productive science is concerned with problems of making. Knowing, doing, and making are not distingushed in the sense that something made, for example, cannot in some way be known or in some way affect what we do. Rather they are distinguished in the sense that each involves a subject matter, a mode of procedure, a criterion, and an end or function which is different in kind from that involved in the other two. A full explanation of the differences between theoretical, practical, and productive science as Aristotle conceived them would carry us beyond the scope of this analysis. But as we follow the argument of the *Poetics* we should be able to see, at least in the case of this work, that it has its own subject matter, method, principle, and function and that these in fact constitute the particular problem at hand. This peculiarity is the essential mark of Aristotle's method in the most general sense of that term.

Because the inquiry is handled problematically, those factors which are relevant to the solution of the problem must be separated from those that are irrelevant. This is the importance of the distinction between substance and accident which Aristotle uses throughout his writings. For what is relevant to the problem at hand is the essential or substantial. The accidental is what is irrelevant, though it might be quite essential to another problem. Problems of art, then, are problems of production, and whatever contributes to our understanding of those problems is essential to art. Everything else is accidental and therefore irrelevant to that discussion.

But however important it may be to point out the peculiarities of Aristotle's method of conducting inquiry, it is not his method which separates his work the most from contemporary aesthetic discussions. For in every age there have been philosophers whose mode of procedure has emphasized the separation of problems. From the contemporary point of view what is most distinctive in Aristotle's approach to aesthetic problems is that the problems are located by means of an investigation of the relations between nature and art. By Aristotle's approach the problems of making are stated and solved in terms of the requirements of the thing that arises from this process, the product or work of art. For the process of making and the product made are essentially the same in the sense that they have the same formula or definition, since the product is simply the end of the process of making, its fulfillment or completion, and the nature of anything is what it is when its genesis is completed. The process, however, cannot be investigated as such. Its nature can only be determined by the examination of its perceptible result, the product. But the product of art, an artificial thing, is identifiable as a work of art, as we shall see below, by its distinction from natural objects. It is, in fact, the essential differences between natural and artificial things that determine the procedure by which Aristotle sets up the whole discussion of tragedy, for it is the peculiarities of artificial things that fix the peculiarities of productive problems. That Aristotle proceeds by *distinguishing* nature from art is an aspect of his method, but that *nature* and *art* are what he distinguishes is a matter of the philosophic fashions of his time.

To anyone conversant with recent discussions on art it might seem a more familiar and more fashionable approach either to treat art (as did the nineteenth century) as a creative process in which the characteristics of art are derived from the creative faculties of the artist, or to regard art (as we tend to do today) as the expression of values communicated to an audience. This is not the place to weigh the merits of these several approaches, if indeed there is any common ground from which they can be judged. But the difference between Aristotle's doctrine and recent tendencies in aesthetic theory must be kept in mind if we are to make an adequate interpretation of his treatise.

If, therefore, problems of art are conceived as problems of making and these can be formulated only by establishing the requirements of the object made, it follows that the first problem to be faced is that of determining the nature of the artificial object. But this nature cannot be the nature of an artificial object in general. One has solved the problems of making only when one has determined what it is to make a *specific* kind of thing. For no one makes a product in general, but only a product of a definite kind, and this is true whether he makes it by luck or by art. For Aristotle, therefore, there can be no general aesthetic which establishes universal laws of art running across the various species of art. What is appropriate to a tragedy is out of place in a comedy, or if it is suitable to both it is by virtue of what they have in common and not by virtue of their peculiar natures. Again, the sort of problems which a composer of a symphony must face are of a completely different kind from those which must be met by a landscape painter. The *Poetics* can give us important clues as to how Aristotle would face other kinds of productive problems, especially those of epic, and to a certain extent those of comedy or even the problems of music, as long as we are sensitive to the differences between those problems and the ones he did work on. But essentially the *Poetics* is a treatise on a single historically evolved species of art, tragedy, and possesses the unity of that specific productive problem. For even the extensive treatment of epic, we shall find, has its place in this discussion primarily because of the concern with tragedy.

The problem of determining the nature of any artificial object such as tragedy is confronted by an immediate difficulty. By Aristotle's approach a "thing," whether natural or artificial, is a structure or synthesis of parts. The unifying structure of the thing is what Aristotle calls its *form*, while the parts are the *material* which is unified by the form. In the case of natural objects there is a dynamic connection between the material parts and their formal interconnection or unity. The form of an oak tree, for example, is simply the interconnection and coherence which the parts of the tree, as parts, possess as a potentiality. The form of the tree exists potentially in the parts in the sense that the parts possess the form as a tendency. For otherwise it would be impossible to explain why acorns never develop into maples. No external cause needs to be, or can be, brought in to explain the coming-to-be of a natural thing, for the form, as latent in the parts, is itself the cause of the thing. This is what Aristotle means in the *Physics* when he says that nature is an internal principle of motion. In nature, therefore, a "thing" is a concrete existent whose material parts possess, in themselves, a power or potentiality which is actualized in their form, and while matter is the potentiality of the thing, the form is its actuality.

But an artificial object is not a "thing" in this strict sense of the term and has no necessary "nature." For as a concrete existent or composite whole of form and matter there is no necessary connection between the material parts of which it is made and the organization of those parts which constitutes its form. A work of art does not have a form which is the actualization of the natural potentiality of its parts. It does not have an internal principle of genesis. Instead its genesis is due to an artist or maker, external to the object, who shapes the material into an organization which the material does not naturally possess. For bronze does not by nature come in the shape of men, and sounds do not naturally occur in the form of symphonies. An object that is made, therefore, not only owes its existence to some external power, but possesses a form obtained from a source in nature other than the material which that form organizes.

The term which Aristotle uses to express the relation between art and nature is *imitation,* for the work of art can be said to imitate the natural object from which its form is derived. The word is also prominent in the writings of Plato, Isocrates, and other Greeks. For imitation is of primary importance whenever aesthetic problems are couched in terms of the relations of art and nature. But the meaning which Aristotle gives to the term is dependent, at least in part, on the peculiarities of his method by which the problems of art and nature are distinguished. That art imitates nature does not mean, as some commentators have assumed, that Aristotle conceived a work of art as a literal copy of nature. First of all, the form which an artist imposes on his materials is not the essential form of the natural object which actualizes the potentiality of its parts, but the perceptible form which is accidental to that essence. A painting of a tree, for example, makes use of the visual form of the tree, not the intellectual form which the botanist understands. If art were merely a copy of nature, then, it would have to be a copy of the accidents of nature, not of its essence. But more important than this, we will see later that even this perceptible form is controlled by a principle which is peculiar to the work of art and is not derived either from the natural object which supplies the perceptible form or from the artist who produces the work. The term imitation, therefore, expresses for Aristotle the criterion by which the problems of art and nature can be distinguished, not collapsed. From what we have said of Aristotle's conception of art we can sum up his notion of imitation as follows: An imitation (e.g. tragedy) is

(1) material (speech), which is given

(2) an organization or form (the actions of men) which the material as such does not naturally possess, by the efficacy of

(3) an external power (the poet), in accordance with

(4) a function or principle which is purely artistic and not derived from theoretical or practical science.

The four aspects of imitation which we have enumerated are the four conditions which in their interconnection or unity define its nature. They are the four "causes" upon which the existence of an imitation depends. In general, the four causes were held by Aristotle to constitute an exhaustive enumeration of the factors which enter into any problem. They are therefore integral to his method. They are, all of them, answers to the question "Why?" For why a thing is what it is (and it makes no difference what mode of existence the thing has) depends on (1) the parts which constitute its material, (2) the form or structure of those parts which give them unity and wholeness. (3) the way in which the material takes on that structure—that is, the source of motion by which the form and matter are brought together to constitute the existing thing, and (4) the function or purpose which the thing attains. These four aspects of any kind of existent thing are called respectively the *material, formal, efficient,* and *final* causes of that thing. Any attempt to solve any problem must account for all four of these aspects of the subject matter if it is to pretend to any completeness and validity, and when these have all been specified the account is complete, at least in outline.

An understanding of the function which the four causes have in inquiry is important to an adequate grasp of Aristotle's procedure. The *Poetics* has often been supposed to be an incomplete treatise, parts of it written at widely spaced intervals of time, and to have little coherence in its structure and the logic of its argument. Since the four causes are exhaustive of the factors which are germane to any problem, they can be used effectively, not only to show the relevance of the various parts of his argument, but also to exhibit the completeness of his statement of the problem. Throughout our analysis of the *Poetics,* therefore, we will make liberal application of these causes in order to articulate his procedure. It should be kept in mind, however, that everything will have its proper causes, including the causes themselves. Thus we will be concerned, not only with the causes of tragedy, but the causes of those causes, and so on. For each cause becomes itself the subject of discussion and must itself be explained by reference to the factors which explain it, until at last the argument is grounded in an ultimate cause or principle which is self-caused or reflexive.* For, as Aristotle argues in the *Posterior Analytics,* the causal chain cannot be infinite. In the discussion that follows, therefore, it will be important to keep the various levels of causes distinct by clearly discerning what it is whose causes are being determined. For the efficient cause of the plot of tragedy, for example, is not the efficient cause of tragedy itself.

To return now to the point at which we digressed, an imitation is not a "thing" in the strict sense of the term, but what we might call a "quasi-thing" having no natural connection between its form and matter. It can therefore have a "nature" only in a secondary and derivative sense of the term, since its nature cannot be considered necessary insofar as its form is not the actualization of the innate tendencies of its materials. That is, a product is not something that arises by nature. It is the result of the efforts of countless artists through long periods of time. For not only do artists make individual tragedies, but they make tragedy itself as a kind of thing. In order to determine the nature of tragedy, therefore, it becomes appropriate to examine the efficient cause of tragedy—that is, the artist who brings about its existence. But since the artist, as maker, is defined by the poetic process by which the work of art is produced (for a maker is one who makes), the examination of the efficient cause of tragedy turns out to be an examination of the process by which tragedy arose as a species of art. This problem of accounting for the genesis of tragedy is undertaken in the first five chapters of the *Poetics.* Chapters 1-5 are therefore an account of the factors or causes which explain the genesis of this species. The

* By Aristotle's method the investigation of a problem is always pursued until a principle is discovered which is not only the cause of the attributes of the thing investigated, but also the starting point of the demonstration of statements about the thing. In the examination of tragedy, as we will see, such a principle is found in the catharsis of pity and fear.

specification of the nature of tragedy is accomplished by tracing the genesis of the species from its beginnings to the point at which the definitory characteristics of tragedy can be discerned. For though it is the product that determines the nature of the process and not vice versa, still by articulating the factors in the process which serve as conditions for the genesis of tragedy, it is possible to observe the rise of the species with its own integrity of form.

II. *The Genesis of Tragedy, Chapters 1-5*

The account of tragedy's genesis has two stages. First Aristotle must determine those factors in the process which exist prior to and independent of its emergence as a thing. The discussion of these antecedent conditions occupies chapters 1-3. Second, there must be an examination of the historical process itself which issues in a definable species. This problem is dealt with in chapters 4 and 5.

The three antecedent causes or conditions of the genesis of art works were distinguished above when the general concept of imitation was explicated. For one of the prior conditions of art is the material upon which the artist works. In chapter 1 the *materials of imitation* are distinguished into their various kinds in order to determine which is appropriate to tragedy. A second antecedent factor is the perceptible natural form which the artist imitates in order to organize his material, and the various forms or *objects of imitation* are distinguished into kinds in chapter 2. Finally, chapter 3 discusses the third antecedent condition of the rise of art, the artist himself as he relates to this process. For the *manner of imitation* which chapter 3 distinguishes into kinds is the way in which the artist, as maker, operates in organizing his materials according to the form he has chosen. Chapters 1-3 thus deal respectively with the material, formal, and efficient causes of

the genesis of tragedy. That these causes are all antecedent to the establishment of any species of art, and
are therefore prior to its nature, means that they represent the latitude which is at the artist's disposal independent of any commitment to a given genre of art. For
this reason they afford a kind of *a priori* classification of
kinds of art works or genres. This is why Aristotle calls
the material, object, and manner of imitation the differentiae of art. For while any kind of art presupposes all
three of these factors, the various kinds of art can be
differentiated according to the specific material, object,
and manner of imitation employed.

The first two paragraphs of chapter 1 set up the discussion of the causes of tragedy's genesis. The first paragraph states in four short clauses the procedure which
the *Poetics* as a whole is to follow. (1) The subject of
discussion is said to be poetic or productive science or
the inquiry into productive problems in general, and
the species of this. (2) Poetic is conceived as a power, and
by this Aristotle means the power to produce products or
works of art. But a power or potentiality cannot be examined save as it is actualized, and the actualization of
a productive power is the concrete organization which is
the product. Therefore, one knows a specific poetic
power only by knowing (3) the construction of the resulting product, and in the case of tragedy this construction or organization is its plot. Finally, this poetic
power can be known only as the interconnection and
unity of its parts are determined, and for this purpose
(4) the parts of the process of making must be distinguished. The four clauses thus establish the subject matter of the treatise and the considerations which determine the method or the way in which Aristotle proposes
to investigate this subject.

The method is to start from "first things," and these,
as the second paragraph indicates, are the three antecedent conditions of making which we have discussed

above. In order to exemplify these three causes and differentiae of the poetic process Aristotle lists, in three groups of two, six of the species of art which had arisen in his day. Epic-making and the making of tragedy are poetic processes which differ in their manner of imitation, since the former imitates in narration while the latter is dramatic. These two in turn differ from the next pair, comedy and dithyrambic art, in the things which they imitate, since the former pair imitate what is worthy or better than average, while the latter imitate what is base or beneath the average. Finally, all four of these differ from the last pair in the materials in which the imitation is produced, since the former use speech, while the arts of the aulos and kithara use the non-significant voice of musical instruments.

The remainder of chapter 1 is devoted to the materials of imitation. There are two major kinds: the visual (which is divisible into color, as in painting, and figure or shape, as in sculpture and architecture) and the auditory (voice). Voice has three dimensions: rhythm, harmony, and speech. Rhythm is the temporal synthesis of voice of which meter is the measure and therefore simply a part. Harmony, in contradistinction to our contemporary meaning, is the ratio between pitches of voice, whether simultaneous or successive. Melody is the synthesis of rhythm and harmony, not simply the ratio of successive pitches as in our contemporary use of the word, for the rhythmic pattern is essential to a melody. Speech is the meaning or significance of voice and distinguishes voice in the strict sense, which is human, from the derivative sense of voice which musical instruments have. Some auditory arts use only one or two of these dimensions of voice, some use all three. Tragedy uses voice in all three senses but not always at the same time.

In the course of his examination of the materials of imitation Aristotle makes a rather important rebuttal to a thesis which stems from an approach to art contrary to his. In the process of distinguishing arts which use different dimensions of voice he states that there is no common name to arts using speech without the adornment of harmony, or what we would today refer to, perhaps, as the literary arts. Nor would we have a common name, he adds, for works using speech without meter (what we would call prose works) or works using the same kind of meter (what we would call kinds of poems), if it were not that some men think that the genera of art are determined simply by the kind of materials used. Aristotle's position is that species of art differ from each other as different kinds of imitations, and there are, as we have seen, four factors or causes which fix a kind of imitation. One cause by itself cannot exhibit the full nature of a species of art, and without this full specification it is impossible to establish it as a unified thing. A classification of kinds according to the material cause alone, therefore, can never distinguish true species, but will only make accidental divisions. The fact that two works of art use meter is no assurance that they have any essential similarity. Of our contemporary distinction between prose and poetry, therefore, Aristotle would say that, while it is of course legitimate to say some literary works use meter and some do not, still poems and works of prose are not *kinds* of art works. For the distinction does not touch their status as *things,* but only what they are made of. To call a thing a poem (not in Aristotle's broad sense of anything made, but in the contemporary sense of a thing using meter as its material) is thus exactly like referring to "a thing made of wood." For there is no more essential sameness to things made of meters than to wooden things, red things, things in this room, things made by Englishmen, or things of the twentieth century. For the specification is in every case by means of something accidental to things as things.

Aristotle's discussion of the object of imitation in chapter 2 starts with the statement that all imitations imitate agents—that is, human beings acting or being acted upon. In chapter 1 the same point is made in connection with dancing when he says that the object imitated is either the actions, passions, or characters of men. These imitated objects are in all cases either better than we are, as we are, or worse. That is, what is imitated is either something worthy and noble, or base and degraded, or perhaps in between. Tragedy imitates what is worthy while comedy imitates what is base though, as he says in chapter 5, painless. As we will see later, the worth of the agents determines the affective meaning of tragedy to be that of pity and fear. And since comedy imitates the ludicrous rather than the worthy, the comic emotions are the contraries of these.

Each art, Aristotle assumes, has its appropriate pleasure which serves as its end or function. What constitutes that pleasure is the emotional or affective meaning of the work. The affective meaning of the work is determined by the moral meaning of the object imitated by that species of art, its goodness or badness, for it is primarily these qualities in things that move us. But if the pleasure of art derives from the moral qualities of what is imitated, then man is what art primarily imitates, for nothing has either moral or affective meaning except in its relation to man. All art imitates human agents, therefore, either by imitating man in the fullest, most concrete sense—that is, man as agent or man as possessing definite traits of character acting or being acted upon in situations determined by agents—or by imitating some aspect of man abstracted from his total being. For a lyric poem imitates man's passions by abstracting these from the larger context of life which serves as the object imitated by drama and narrative. Painting makes an even further abstraction when it imitates, not the characters themselves of men, but the visual signs of those characters found in facial appearance or bodily condition. Or at a further remove from agents in the complete sense, it may give us the signs of human feeling in the mood that pervades a landscape or even a non-objective organization of lines or colors.

At the extreme of this abstractive process the moral significance is no longer clear, and in fact even the feelings become so generalized that they are difficult to discern. But it is still the feeling or affective significance of a work of art that gives form to its proper pleasure; and the greatest significance, and therefore the greatest pleasure, lies not in what is most generalized, but in the specific emotions articulated by objects which retain their moral dimensions. The form of any work of art will therefore be specifiable according to its affective significance. For it is not simply action, or character, or thought *as such* that gives form to a work of art, but an action, a character, or a thought *of a given sort,* and the only meaningful way of distinguishing these sorts is in terms of their affective significance.

Chapter 3 is concerned with the manner of imitation or the way in which the artist, as artist, gives his materials the perceptible form of some natural object. The manner of imitation thus involves the question of the moving or efficient cause of the process by which imitations are generated—that is, the process by which a material is changed to a new form. The distinction between kinds of manner which Aristotle gives (i.e. narrative versus dramatic imitation) appears to be one which is pertinent only to the literary arts. But the way in which Aristotle makes the distinction should give us a clue as to its wider application. For a work is said to be narrative if the poet himself is the agency in the production of the work, while it is dramatic if the work involves a production by his agent. This comes out most clearly, perhaps, in chapter 6 when Aristotle accounts for spectacle as one of the formal parts of tragedy and, in fact, that part which relates to tragedy's manner of imitation. For tragedy has spectacle because the poet has agents who do the actual making or producing of the play, and by agents he means the actors who get out on the stage and act. To put it in more general terms, the material, voice, is not his own, but that of someone who represents him and who does as he directs. In narration the words are the voice of the poet, and even if he should at times assume the role of one he talks about, nevertheless it is the poet who assumes that role. An analogous distinction can be made for music, for the musical instrument becomes the representative of the poet's voice, so that instrumental music is to vocal music as dramatic poetry is to narrative. And it is clear from the universality of his statements that Aristotle thought that comparable distinctions in manner could be made in the case of the plastic or visual arts. In general, therefore, the manner of imitation involves the question of whether or not the artist, as artist, intrudes himself upon his work—that is, whether he produces the work with or without the identification in his work of his role as maker.

The three antecedent causes of the imitating process, in conjunction but not separately, serve as differentiae of this process by which an *a priori* classification of works of art into species can be effected. The order in which these causes are considered is from the more general and disparate to the more specific and closely related. That is, tragedy is more widely separated from the plastic arts (a distinction of material), less separated from comedy (a distinction of form), but closely related to epic (a distinction of manner); for, as chapter 26 states, tragedy and epic have the same function—namely, the catharsis of pity and fear. In general, the order is determined by the nature of the poetic genre toward whose definition the discussion leads. Presumably in the inves-

tigation of some other species of art these three antecedent causes would be discussed in a different order if
the nature of the species so determined it.

That the three antecedent causes of the genesis of
tragedy (speech, worthy actions, and dramatization) effect its classification among arts, does not mean, how
ever, that they are sufficient for its definition. For to
define is to show the unity of the factors which constitute a thing, and whatever unifies or controls the intrinsic properties of a thing cannot be found in its antecedent conditions or else those properties cannot be
intrinsic. Classification, in fact, can only be a propaedeutic to the investigation of problems, for classification
serves merely to isolate the subject of discussion so that
inquiry can proceed. It creates problems rather than
solves them. To arrive at the definition of tragedy it
is necessary to survey the history of its genesis, for from
this survey the properties of the thing can be seen to
rise as the accidents are discarded, and by what may be
called an intellectual penetration of these properties
(an act of thought discussed in the *Posterior Analytics*)
their principle can be discerned. For, as Aristotle says
in chapter 14, the genesis of a species of art first proceeds by fortune, not by art. This is in fact obvious if
art is a productive process aiming at an end, for as long
as the species itself is being generated this end is as yet
undetermined. Observation of the trials and errors which
constitute the evolution of a species thus directs one to
the defining characteristics of that species.*

The attempt to fix the properties which are attrib-
utable of tragedy as a form has stages which can be

* It is important to notice, in spite of widespread opinion
to the contrary, that Aristotle's general procedure of attacking
problems of science in terms of the definitions of species does
not preclude the possibility of the evolution of those species,
although it is doubtful that it occurred to Aristotle that
natural species did evolve.

distinguished in the three paragraphs of chapter 4. The three stages of the discussion correspond to three aspects of the generated species, each of which has its proper cause. The first paragraph finds a general cause, innate in man, which accounts for the genesis, not of tragedy alone, but of the process of making or imitating in general. This cause is man's pleasure in imitation. This pleasure can be viewed either from the standpoint of the maker (for there is pleasure in making) or from that of the audience (for there is pleasure in viewing imitations). In either case the pleasure arises from the fact that imitations are a source of learning. But by learning Aristotle cannot mean the acquisition of theoretical or practical science. That is, what we gain from making or viewing imitations *as imitations* are not the truths of nature or the habits and institutions which arise from practice. This interpretation would destroy the problematic separation of the sciences which is integral to Aristotle's method by dialectically reducing all science to one hierarchy of knowledge.

In the *Metaphysics,* Book VII, Chap. 7, Aristotle states that the genesis of a product has two parts. One is an intellectual activity whereby from the assumption of a given end (i.e. the form to be produced) one reasons out the requisites to this end. The second part is the making which proceeds in the contrary direction, from that which can first be done and is the terminus of the intellectual activity, to the completion of the end or form. Making is thus not itself thought, but is in accordance with thought. The learning that is essential and not accidental to production will therefore have two aspects. One concerns the comprehension or understanding of the form and function which constitutes the essence of. the product, the other concerns the grasp of the relations of the parts to that end which necessitates them. The delight which is gained from the contemplation of an imitation, as imitation, therefore consists in learning and reasoning out the unity of form which the parts achieve.* And should this form (the object of imitation) elude the contemplation, then the pleasure will derive from the execution (the manner of imitation) or from such causes as the color or the harmony and rhythm (the material of imitation).

The second paragraph of chapter 4 accounts for the genesis, not of the process of making generally, but of the two general kinds of imitating distinguished according to the affective significance of what is imitated. The historical separation of the process of making into that which imitates the noble and that which imitates the base is traced, not to an innate tendency in all men, but to a dispositional difference among men lying in their characters. The cause of the separation of making into kinds is thus of an entirely different kind than that which accounts for making in general. It is a cause found at a further remove from man's general nature and closer to the peculiarities of the work of art, for the character of the maker to which the affective qualities of the imitation are related is something acquired and not innate.

Finally, the third paragraph accounts for the genesis of tragedy, not as an imitation in general (as does paragraph one), and not as an imitation possessing one of two kinds of affective qualities (as does paragraph two), but as an imitation of a specific and definable kind. Furthermore, the cause of tragedy's specific properties is found, not in the innate tendencies of men, nor in their acquired dispositions, but in the appropriateness of those properties to a function or form which rises only improvisationally and more by fortune than by art.

* Though this delight is said to be innate it is not a property of man—that is, the sort of thing which psychology would determine as essential to man's nature. For this delight is an extrinsic attribute of man, i.e. it is a relation between man and something external to him and therefore cannot be attributed of man as such.

That is, the characteristics which tragedy exhibits when it has attained its nature are ultimately determined by the artistic function which constitutes that nature,* and not by the peculiarities of extrinsic conditions. The properties which tragedy exhibits as an artistic form are listed under three heads and are observed by contrasting tragedy with the dithyramb, a species of art achieving an entirely different function, from which historically tragedy arose.

Chapter 5, on the other hand, searches, not for those properties of tragedy which relate to its nature as a whole as determined by the uniqueness of its function, but for those properties which the parts of tragedy exhibit in independence of its function. Appropriately, these properites are found by contrasting tragedy, not with a species of art unrelated except for the accidents of history, but with epic, a species which attains a function identical to that of tragedy. Again, the properties found are listed under three heads.

The historical survey of the genesis of tragedy in chapters 4 and 5 thus culminates in two contrasting procedures by which the data necessary to the examination of tragedy are gathered and articulated. In the third paragraph of chapter 4 the identity of parts in dithyramb and tragedy (by virtue of which the potentiality of the rise of tragedy from dithyramb is to be explained) allows Aristotle to focus on those properties of tragedy relating to the peculiarity of its functional wholeness. In the second paragraph of chapter 5 the identity of the function of epic and tragedy allows him to focus on the properties of tragedy relating to the

---

* The efficient cause of tragedy is thus determined ultimately to be the nature of tragedy itself, for if the poet is this efficient cause he is such only by virtue of a power which is identical in formula or definition with the nature of the product.

peculiarity of its parts. This two-fold historical procedure illustrates the peculiarities of the role which history
plays in the philosophy of Aristotle. For history by his
problematic method is simply the material data relevant
to the solution of a problem found in some science. It
is the problem which determines what constitutes data
relevant to its solution; and therefore the fashion in
which the facts are organized, even for statement, must
reflect the way in which the problem articulates itself.
Ultimately, therefore, no essential difference exists between history and science, for when the facts are assem-
bled in their relevance to the problem and their interrelations are established the problem is solved and
science is attained. History is therefore the potentiality
of which science is the actuality.

In summary, then, chapters 1-5, which form the first
of the three main divisions of the *Poetics*, constitute an
examination of the genesis of tragedy. That is, they examine tragedy from the standpoint of the moving or
efficient cause which brings form and matter together
to produce the composite whole which is tragedy considered as an imitation. They are, in fact, an examination of the function of the artist who is this efficient
cause of the work of art, for the power which defines
the artist as maker is exactly the power which is actualized in this process. Chapters 1-5 are, if you will, Aristotle's version of the problem of creativity—the problem which absorbed aestheticians during the eighteenth
and nineteenth centuries. With Aristotle, however, the
consideration of the creative process is subordinate to the
consideration of art as imitation, a kind of existing
thing. For the discussion of the efficient cause of tragedy
is necessary, as we will see, as a propaedeutic to the
primary aesthetic problem found in the relation of the
formal and material causes of tragedy. For the actualization of the poetic power, whose genesis is traced in chap-

ters 1-5, is the composite whole of form and matter, and for the specification of tragedy's nature as an imitation these two causes are sufficient.

III. *The Definition of Tragedy and Its Formal Parts, Chapter 6*

Chapters 6-22 form the second of the three main divisions of the *Poetics*. They constitute the most important of these divisions, since it is here that Aristotle addresses himself to his primary aesthetic problem, the determination of the nature of tragedy conceived as imitation. This problem is primary in the sense that it controls the treatment of tragedy as making or creating in chapters 1-5 and the treatment of tragedy as expression in the final division, chapters 23-26. As an imitation or composite whole, tragedy is viewed as an organization or structure imposed upon material parts. The discussion of tragedy as a thing in chapters 6-22 must therefore turn on the relationship established between tragedy's formal and material causes. Appropriately, chapters 7-18 are concerned with the formal cause of tragedy, while chapters 19-22 are concerned with its material cause.* The function of chapter 6 is to articulate the considerations which determine this manner of structuring the problem.

The definition of tragedy with which chapter 6 begins is said by Aristotle to be gathered up from the preceding discussion, i.e. chapters 1-5. The definition of tragedy is thus the fruition of the inquiry into its efficient cause. The definition falls immediately into four parts, each of which is traceable to the preceding discussion. These four parts constitute the four causes of tragedy's nature. The object of imitation or formal cause (discussed in

---

* Chapters 1-5, as we have seen, treat of tragedy as an efficient cause; and, as we will see later, chapters 23-26 treat of tragedy as a function or end in the expression of a poetic idea, i.e. as final cause.

chapter 2) is "worthy and complete action having magnitude." The material cause or that in which the imitation is produced (discussed in chapter 1) is "speech
made pleasing"—that is, speech with the ornamentations
of rhythm, harmony, and melody used in various parts.
The manner of imitation or the characteristic which
tragedy has in respect of its efficient cause (discussed in
chapter 3) consists in its being "performed and not produced through narration." The function or proper pleasure which constitutes the final cause of tragedy consists
in its "achieving through pity and fear a catharsis of
such affections." It was for the purpose of ascertaining
this function that the historical survey of the essential
properties of tragedy was made in chapters 4 and 5. For
with the determination of these properties gained
through the comparison of tragedy with the dithyramb
and the epic, the mind, as we have said above, is in a
position to grasp by an intellectual penetration of these
properties the ultimate cause on which they depend.
That is to say, the inductive process culminates in an
immediate act of the understanding in which the principle of tragedy is apprehended. This principle then
becomes, as we shall see, the starting point of the argument by which discursively reason can demonstrate those
properties, for it is this principle or end which is the
ground of their necessity. It is therefore the attainment
of the principle of catharsis that makes possible a scientific treatment of poetic or productive problems. For
without the principle the inquirer has only the facts of
tragedy, yet without the reason for the facts he cannot
be sure they are the facts.

It is imperative to compare this four-part definition
of tragedy with the two-part definition consisting of
genus and differentia which Aristotle regards as appropriate to theoretical science. The four-part definition
found in productive science is a statement of the four
conditions under which an object, having no necessary

nature, obtains its being. A natural object of theoretical science is what it is by being simply a further specification of something that already has a natural existence, and therefore to determine its nature it is sufficient to state the kind of thing it is (its genus) and how it differs from other things of this kind (its differentia).

Of these four parts of the definition, three refer to the antecedent conditions of art. These are the object imitated (worthy action), the material which is organized (ornamented speech), and the manner in which the poet effects that organization (by dramatization). Only the function or end of tragedy, the catharsis of pity and fear, is not prior to the construction. Yet all four are equally internal to tragedy, whether tragedy be considered as a process of making or a thing made. In fact the first three parts of the definition determine the six formal parts of tragedy: plot, character, thought, diction, melody, and spectacle. Plot, character, and thought are formal parts as a consequence of the fact that the object imitated is the actions of agents. Diction and melody are formal parts as a consequence of the fact that the material which is organized is ornamented speech. Spectacle is a formal part as a consequence of the fact that the manner by which the imitation is produced consists in the appearance on stage of agents (actors) who literally make the action, albeit as representatives of the poet.

Aristotle sharply distinguishes between such terms as action, agent, and speech, which refer to things even as they exist independently of art; and the six terms just enumerated, which refer to formal parts of the work itself. For the six parts of tragedy are all constructions of the poet, while the other terms all refer to antecedent conditions of art. Plot, for example, is not the same as action, but is instead the imitation of action, and so with the rest. The dependence of the six formal parts on the antecedent conditions of art is exactly what is meant by saying that art imitates nature, or that the form imposed on the material is derived from nature. Yet once the formal parts have been determined the antecedent generating conditions can be ignored. For, as we shall see later on, the result of those conditions is a self-subsisting entity, the work of art, and within that artificial entity can be found the criterion for the adequacy of any statements made about it—namely, the catharsis of pity and fear.

The relationships established in chapter 6 between the six parts of tragedy set up the organization of the second main division of the *Poetics*. The parts are given an order according to a hierarchy from the "greatest" to the "least." In this hierarchy a difference can be noted between the way in which plot, character, thought, and diction are related to each other and the way in which melody and spectacle are related to those four. Let us take the first group first.

The antecedent material on which the poet works is voice. According to chapter 1 voice has three constituent parts—speech, rhythm, and harmony: or simply speech and melody, since melody is the synthesis or organization of rhythm and harmony in the Greek sense of these terms. But since melody is simply the pleasing ornamentation of speech, it is speech which is the primary antecedent material in which poetic diction is produced. In chapter 6 Aristotle refers to diction as the "synthesis of meters" and as "interpretation through language." Since he says he regards the second phrase as the equivalent of the first, he must mean that to synthesize meters is to establish relations between words and that these relations constitute the interpretation of what the words individually signify—that is, the things of which the words are signs. Diction is therefore an artifact or poetic construction consisting in an organization of speech through the poetic interpretation of words. As an organization imposed by art on a material diction is thus a formal part, i.e. a form, in exactly the same sense as the other five parts of tragedy.

But diction is not the organization of speech into propositions. For according to chapter 20, the materials whose synthesis constitutes diction range from indivisible voice (whose sign is the letter of the alphabet) to speech which is defined as synthesized significant voice, not necessarily containing verbs. And in chapter 21 the highest form of diction is found to be the metaphor, which is simply the "transfer of a word belonging to something else." To make such a transference is not to predicate, and it is predication which is the essential condition of propositions. The function of synthesizing diction so as to effect propositions or arguments is expressly affirmed of thought, for thought is said to exist "in whatever agents say when demonstrating something or declaring some consideration" or, again, "thought exists in those speeches in which the speakers demonstrate that something is or is not the case or declare something universal." There are therefore two ways in which diction can be synthesized or organized. One is thought in the discursive sense which we call reasoning. The other is thought in the immediate or intuitive sense which we call understanding. The immediate synthesis or organization of diction, then, is thought, for words put together to form unities are thoughts, either in the sense of understandings or in the sense of reasonings. Thought therefore is the end to which diction is means, and thought stands to diction as form to matter.

Characters are said to be "the things by virtue of which we say the agents are of a certain kind." For this reason they "make the choice evident—that is, what sort of action is chosen or avoided in cases not evident in themselves—and on this account those speeches do not possess character which do not in a general way include what the speaker chooses or avoids." For speeches to include "in a general way" what is chosen or avoided must mean that the thought contained in the choice must be related to a general tendency and this establishes of what sort the agent is, i.e. his character. Character is thus the organization of thought, for it is character which relates thoughts to a unity. Therefore, just as thought is the form of diction, so character is the form of otherwise separate thoughts, and in this latter relation thought is a material rather than a form.

Finally, characters would remain separated and out of relation except for their interrelations through action. And since plot is the imitation of action and "the synthesis of incidents," it must stand to characters as character does to thoughts and as thought does to diction. As the "synthesis of incidents," plot is the concrete unity of every "occurrence" in the play. It therefore does not mean for Aristotle, as it does for many contemporary writers, the bare skeleton or synopsis of what happens. His term for the synopsis or outline, as we will see, is argument, not plot. To give the plot would mean for Aristotle to produce the play in its entirety, not to give its outline. Nor would it be meaningful in his sense of the term to speak of a play as having more than one plot, for the plot is simply the way in which every incident finds relation to every other. Plot is therefore the form of all the other formal parts and is the ultimate end to which they are means, for it is the requirements of plot which determine what kinds of characters, thoughts, and diction ought to be included. As their ultimate cause or principle it is "the soul of tragedy." Diction, thought, character, and plot thus constitute an ascending hierarchy of more inclusive forms in which the lower syntheses are means to the attainment of the higher and in which the higher are the organizations or unities of the lower. In this hierarchy plot is the ultimate organization or form, while diction is the ultimate matter, or that which ultimately is organized.

Melody and spectacle, however, are not related to each other or to the other four parts in quite the same way. These two parts Aristotle calls the ornaments or pleasing accessories of tragedy. As ornaments they will be determined ultimately by the requirements of the plot, and in this sense they are materials on which the higher forms impose an organization. That is to say, what melodies are needed to ornament the diction will be determined by the interpretation desired, the thought expressed, who expresses it, and under what circumstances. So also spectacle, which is simply the visual aspect of the drama, the scenery, costumes, gestures, etc., will be determined by the requirements of the action represented. But diction obviously cannot be regarded as the synthesis of melody in the sense in which thought is the synthesis of diction. Nor can melody in any sense be the synthesis of spectacle—that is, its unity or form. The relation of melody and spectacle to the other formal parts is therefore of an entirely different order, and this relation is expressed by Aristotle in the term ornament or pleasing accessory. Melody is the ornament of diction or tragedy's ultimate poetic material, while spectacle is the ornament of plot or tragedy's ultimate poetic form.

Attention has already been drawn to the fact that Aristotle's treatment of tragedy as an imitation means that the fundamental problems of art are stated in terms of the requirements imposed upon material parts by an organic unity or form to which those parts serve as means. Tragedy will have been explicated, therefore, when the nature of this form and the potentialities of the material parts in respect of this form have been established. But we have already seen that tragedy, considered as a composite whole, i.e. as an enmattered form or concrete entity, has no necessary nature and is in fact a thing only in a derivative sense of the term. The problem then is how any discussion of it as form and matter can determine it to be a thing, even in a derivative sense.

'The answer to this problem will show the great importance of the first five chapters of the *Poetics* when the generating conditions of tragedy were discussed. For, as we have seen, the ultimate poetic form of tragedy (its plot) and its ultimate poetic material (diction) have their antecedent conditions respectively in an object of imitation (the noble actions of men) and in materials in which the imitation is produced (speech or human voice in respect of its significance), for these latter two exist prior to and not because of tragedy. The artificial nature of tragedy can be determined, as artificial and as a nature, if the formal parts of tragedy (plot, character, thought, diction, melody, and spectacle) can be shown to arise from these two prior conditions, and yet to achieve an integrity of form independent of these conditions from which they arise.

Now melody and spectacle have been shown to be ornaments, important in their own right, but not constitutive of tragedy's nature, since they are determined by the other formal parts. Character and thought have been shown to be intermediate forms rising out of the potentialities of diction and determined by the requirements of plot. It therefore follows that these four formal parts of tragedy will have been accounted for if tragedy's ultimate poetic form and tragedy's ultimate poetic matter, plot and diction, can be accounted for. That is, if plot can be shown to rise out of the object imitated, but in accordance with an internal poetic principle and not a principle derived from the nature of human actions, and if diction can be shown to rise out of the potentialities of human speech, but in accordance with an internal poetic principle and not a principle derived from the nature of human speech, then the "nature" of tragedy as a self-subsistent though completely artificial whole will have been established. The problem of demonstrating the nature of tragedy as a "thing," then, involves a demonstration of its independence from its antecedent condition at precisely the two points at which it is most closely related to those conditions. These two points are the extreme poles of the form-matter continuum we discovered between plot, character, thought, and diction. Accordingly, chapters 7-18 are concerned with the four senses in which tragedy has an organization or plot, while chapters 19-22 are concerned with the four aspects of diction as a poetic material whose potentialities can be so organized. And in each of these two sections the chapters are organized toward a demonstration of the independence of the formal part discussed from the antecedent condition to which it is related.

IV. *Plot as Structural Organization, Chapters 7-11*

Chapters 7-18 are divided into four sections which treat of the problems relating to the four causes of plot. Chapters 7-11 deal with the structural unity of plot (its formal cause) and find the principle of that structure in the likelihood and necessity of the incidents. Chapter 12 deals with plot as a quantitative organization (its material cause) and finds the principle of this organization in the unity of the agon. Chapters 13-16 deal with plot as a functional organization achieving tragedy's proper pleasure (its final cause) and find the principle of this functional organization in the catharsis of pity and fear. Finally, chapters 17 and 18 deal with the organization of tragedy as determined by the peculiarities of the poet's intention (the efficient cause of plot) and find the principle of this determination in the poet's argument or poetic idea that he is seeking to express.

The examination in chapters 7-11 of plot as a formal structure or unity of incidents falls in turn into four parts, each of which deals with one of the four causes of that unity. Chapter 7 is concerned with the formal cause of the structure, its order and magnitude. Chapter 8 is concerned with the materials or parts which are given that order and magnitude—namely, the incidents of the plot. Chapter 9 is concerned with the relation of the poet to the structure as its efficient cause and determines the latitude within which he may effect its unity. Finally, chapters 10 and 11 are concerned with the structure of the plot in terms of its end or final cause. It will be noticed that in each chapter the problem of the chapter is solved by an appeal to the same principle—namely, likelihood and necessity. These terms are never defined in the *Poetics*, yet their meaning is essential to an understanding of Aristotle's theory of tragedy. Before going on with analysis of these chapters, therefore, we will try to interpret these terms in a way consistent with his employment of them.

Both likelihood and necessity are conceived by Aristotle as relations between the incidents of the plot as they emerge in time. They are not simple properties of incidents which can be grasped apart from those temporal relations which incidents have to each other. From a given point of time in the sequence only those incidents which have not occurred can be called likely, and only those which have already occurred can be called necessary. For no present moment reveals either the necessity of future incidents or the likelihood of past incidents. Furthermore, as chapter 9 indicates, likelihood and necessity are both species of the possible or potential. For present incidents make both future and past incidents potential, but in different senses. The potentiality or possibility which the present reveals in respect of the future is the likelihood which the present gives to the future. For present incidents show that future incidents are the likely results of the present. The potentiality or possibility which the present reveals in respect of the past is the necessity which the present gives to the past. For present incidents show that past incidents are the necessary conditions of the present. In other words, present incidents are the reasons why future incidents *might* come to be as well as the reasons why past incidents *had* to come to be.

Likelihood and necessity are therefore relations between incidents which structure their coming-to-be and passing-away through time.* To the extent that each incident looks backward to establish necessities and forward to establish likelihoods every moment of the ongoing sequence is ultimately related to every other moment, preceding or following. And it is only by virtue of this dynamic interrelation of the incidents of the plot that the whole sequence attains a structure. For the interrelations of the incidents through likelihood and necessity are what link them all to a common origin in the past and a common end in the future. Likelihood and necessity cannot themselves, however, establish such a beginning or completion. For the necessary conditions of the present can be extended indefinitely into the past as the likely results of the present can be extended indefinitely into the future. Likelihood and necessity can only establish the sequence, they cannot terminate it. What ultimately determines the beginning and completion of the flow of incidents, as we will see in section VI, is the catharsis of pity and fear.

The structural principle of likelihood and necessity, therefore, is a purely poetic principle. It is not what is likely and necessary in nature that gives the plot its poetic structure. For what is likely and necessary in the actions of men may well fail of this criterion when the poet attempts to convey these actions in the medium or material of his art. As we have seen in our explication

* To say that incidents in the structure of a plot rise from necessity and with likelihood is thus quite analogous to Aristotle's statements in the *Physics* that physical or natural events arise "from necessity" or "for the most part." For in physics also, while present events can show the necessity of the past as conditions of the present, they can only show for the most part what the future will be.

of the concept of imitation, the object imitated has its own natural material. When the artist imitates this object he renders its form (its perceptible form) in a different material, whether this be poetic language, musical tone, color, or anything else. It is because this poetic material has potentialities different from those of the natural material of the object imitated that what is likely or necessary in nature is not necessarily what is likely or necessary in art. What must justify the structure of a work of art as art must be the inevitability or believability which art itself is able to attain. For man only *imitates* nature. What he *produces* is art. This is why Aristotle can say in chapter 25 that the artist is free to choose as his object of imitation either what is true, what men suppose to be true, or what ought to be true. For any of these can be rendered believable by art. And the believable in matters of art, as Aristotle shows in chapter 9, is what the artist has rendered likely and necessary within the work.

The principle of likelihood and necessity is also one principle in spite of the fact that the two terms might indicate that two criteria are involved. For the two terms simply reflect the two ways in which a single criterion of appropriateness is fulfilled according to whether the sequence of incidents is viewed from a given moment in time forward to incidents still unrealized, or from that same moment in time backward to incidents already actualized. The two terms thus exhibit the two essential aspects of the reflexive fashion in which incidents bring themselves to at least the unity of a sequence. For the unity or wholeness of plot, as far as its structural sequence is concerned, is the result of the reflexive operation of each incident in pulling together earlier and later incidents so as to make the unity or interconnection of the sequence a function of every stage of the sequence. In other words, likelihood and necessity is a reflexive principle in the sense that it shows that the structural unity of the incidents is a function of those incidents themselves.

In chapter 7 the problem is to determine the formal aspects of the plot's structure. The form of the structure consists in the fact that the sequence of incidents must be a whole or unity which has magnitude or length, and such a whole must have a beginning, middle, and completion. In the flow of incidents that one is the beginning of the sequence which is not shown to arise out of the necessity of any other incident in the sequence. That is, the beginning cannot show any other incident in the sequence to be its condition. Nor can any other incident show the beginning to be likely. Other incidents, however, will rise naturally out of it. That is, other incidents will rise with the likelihoods established by the beginning and will in turn show the necessity of the beginning. Completion and middle are defined analogously. What is important in the definitions is that the termini of the sequence are defined functionally as they establish structure, not according to the order in which they rise for the spectator, which may or may not be the same order. Furthermore, the order of the structure is determinable only by recourse to the logically prior concept of likelihood and necessity which thereby operates as the principle of the order. Incidents are "natural" from a poetic standpoint, therefore, not if they correctly copy the course of nature, but if they arise in accordance with this principle to achieve the "nature" of a plot. The same criterion is again applied in respect of magnitude in the second paragraph. For though the length of the sequence finds a criterion (qualified by reference to the audience) in the need to be seen or remembered as a whole, it is determined (without such qualification) by what is needed to make the sequence likely and necessary.

Chapter 8 is concerned with the problem of the material cause of the structure—that is, the problem of what incidents are to be included in the sequence and what are not. Again Aristotle rejects extra-poetical considerations. For since art does not literally copy nature but only imitates it, it is not what is imitated that decides this issue, but rather the requirement that the incidents be likely and necessary. For an incident that makes evident neither the likelihood nor the necessity of any other incident in the sequence is no part of the sequence.

In chapter 9 the problem is to determine the function of the poet in bringing his sequence to a structural unity. The problem therefore concerns the efficient cause through which a sequence of incidents is given its proper order and magnitude. The four causes of this function of the poet are discussed in the four paragraphs of the chapter.

In the first paragraph the problem is to determine the kind or form of incidents of which the poet is to speak in giving structure to the sequence. While the historian speaks of what has actually come to pass, the poet is concerned with the incidents that are simply possible, whether or not they have actually occurred. What has actually occurred is something particular, but what might occur is a certain kind of thing, something universal, of which there might be innumerable particular examples. The form of incidents of which the poet speaks in structuring the sequence of his plot thus puts his function somewhere between that of the historian who seeks the particularity of actual events and that of the philosopher or scientist who seeks universality in his statements about existing things. For the universality which the poet seeks is simply the universality of the possible—that is, the likelihoods and necessities of certain kinds of characters in certain kinds of situations. It is this form of his incidents, their possibility or potentiality, that guides the poet in making choices when establishing the structure of the plot.

In the second paragraph Aristotle turns to the question of what materials at the poet's disposal are suitable when it is the possible rather than the actual of which he speaks. Oddly enough, it turns out that for this very purpose it is the actual which often best fulfills the need. For what is actual, either in characters or in incidents, must be possible and what is possible is believable. Actual incidents are therefore already in themselves potentially the likely and the necessary.

In the third paragraph are considered the problems involved in the employment of artistic skill to achieve the form of possibility in the incidents and characters chosen. For either the irrelevant desires of the performers or the absence of skill on the part of the poet can result in his choosing materials which fail of likelihood and necessity. If the flow of incidents lacks a real beginning and completion, the plot, as we will see later, is called simple rather than complex (literally, woven together). This, in a sense, is itself a mark of inferior skill. But, as we have already seen, even without a real beginning and completion the incidents can still be related with likelihood and necessity. If the poet also fails to establish these relations between incidents the plot is called episodic. As Aristotle says in chapter 8, such incidents form no part of a sequence.

Finally, the last paragraph of chapter 9 is concerned with a structural function which the poet is able to achieve by the way in which he gives order to his incidents. Aristotle starts the discussion by recalling that the affective significance of the incidents in tragedy are those of pity and fear. Such affective meaning is heightened if the poet makes future incidents likely on the basis of preceding incidents, but does not allow the likelihood of the future incidents to become apparent until they actually occur. For in this way the believability and the affective meaning of the future incidents are made to appear at the same time so that they reinforce one another. In general if an incident occurs without previous incidents establishing its likelihood, it is "the contrary of what would seem to follow"—that is, it is unexpected or unlikely. There are two forms of the unexpected mentioned by Aristotle. The most important is the wondrous, mentioned here. The other is the astounding, which he mentions later. The wondrous is any unexpected incident which was previously desired by a character. The astounding is an unexpected incident which is not related to any previous plan or purpose of a character. The wondrous is therefore related to fortune, for when something unlikely to happen is desired and it actually does come about the result is fortune. The astounding, on the other hand, is related to chance, for when something unlikely happens which is not related to purpose the result is chance. But if the unexpected (whether wondrous or astounding) is made to appear, when it appears, as the likely consequence of the preceding incidents, then the poet has made the incident more wondrous or astounding by establishing the likelihood of the unlikely. For incidents are most wondrous and most astounding if they are not anticipated by previous incidents, yet appear to be the natural consequences of what proceeds once they have occurred. For Aristotle, therefore, instead of the unexpected being by its nature opposed to the principle of likelihood and necessity, it is rather given its highest perfection through the poet's adherence to that principle. Where the wondrous and the astounding do not achieve likelihood they arise episodically, by fortune or by chance. Aristotle gives an example of the wondrous arising by fortune in the story of the statue of Mitys.

In these four paragraphs of chapter 9, therefore, Aristotle is concerned with the problem of the role of the poet in bringing the incidents of his sequence to a proper order and magnitude. That is, chapter 9 is concerned with the efficient cause through which the structure determined in chapter 7 is given to the appropriate materials discussed in chapter 8. The four paragraphs discuss in turn the four factors or causes of this process which the poet controls. Paragraph one is concerned with the formal criterion (the possible) which the poet employs in structuring his incidents. Paragraph two is concerned with the materials appropriate to this form. Paragraph three is concerned with problems relating to the artistic skill necessary to bring this about. Paragraph four is concerned with an end or function (the wondrous and the astounding) which the poet can achieve by the way in which he gives his incidents the form of possibility.

In chapters 10 and 11 the structure of the incidents is viewed as it is related to its end, the function of tragedy or the catharsis of pity and fear.* It has already been shown that the principle of likelihood and necessity is not sufficient to account for the beginning and completion of the sequence of incidents. What accounts for these termini is not the structural relation between the incidents but the function or significance which these incidents attain. This function is examined in chapters 13-16. Yet the beginning and completion are still aspects of tragedy's structure, and even if the structural principle of likelihood and necessity cannot itself account for them, still whatever does account for them must subserve the principle of structure to the extent that it is an aspect of structure. This is shown in chapter 10 when Aristotle distinguishes between simple and complex plots. The simple plot has only the unity af-

* In chapters 10 and 11 Aristotle employs many terms which depend for their full meaning on statements which he makes only in later chapters. Since it would be impossible to give an adequate meaning to these terms unless the problems treated in sections VI and VII of this analysis were discussed here, some parts of this section may appear unclear. The reader is asked to bear with these parts and to return to them after he has read sections VI and VII, at which time the meaning should be more evident.

forded by the likelihood and necessity of its incidents. It does not achieve a complete catharsis. The complex plot, on the other hand, attains catharsis in the fullest sense because it has reversal or recognition or both. At least one of these parts of plot is required, as we will see in section VI, if the sequence of incidents is to have termini that are more than accidental. But neither reversal nor recognition can give the sequence a true beginning and completion unless they arise with likelihood or necessity. For though reversal and recognition are the two most essential factors in tragedy's catharsis of pity and fear, they cannot give this function to the sequence unless they are a part of the sequence.

Having distinguished plots or sequences of incidents into simple and complex according to whether or not the sequence has an essential beginning and completion, Aristotle then examines in chapter 11 the three parts of plot: reversal, recognition, and suffering. For the presence or absence of these parts determines the sense in which the succession of incidents has a beginning and completion. All three of these parts may be present in a complex plot, though as we will see they need not all be. A simple plot can have only suffering, for suffering does not give the plot an essential beginning and completion, and some simple plots, as we will see from chapter 18, do not even have this. As far as Aristotle's definitions of these parts are concerned, it should be noted that a reversal is defined as a change to the contrary in the *action* of a character. Suffering, on the other hand, is simply what happens to a character through an external agency. It is not anything he does. In the fullest sense a reversal is not simply a fall of fortune, but a fall brought on by the very character who suffers the fall. Reversal and recognition may be called active parts of the plot, while suffering is its passive part. For recognitions also are what characters do, not things done to them. This distinction between plot as active and passive will be important when we come to chapter 18.

Chapters 7-11, then, deal with the formal cause or structure of the plot. They deal therefore with only one factor in plot. For the principle of likelihood and necessity can account only for the relations that are established between the incidents of the plot apart from the significance or meaning which they convey. Chapters 7-11 therefore deal with a problem that tragedy shares with comedy. For the difference between these two species of art does not lie primarily in their formal structure, since likelihood and necessity is the formal principle in both of them. Their difference lies rather in the affective function which each attains. In fact, likelihood and necessity might well be used with slight modifications of meaning as the term standing for the structural principle of any work of art synthesized in time, such as narrative works, lyric poetry, or even musical compositions. In the case of art works synthesized spatially rather than temporally, such as paintings and sculpture, the term would perhaps be inappropriate, but by Aristotle's approach to art something analogous would be found to interrelate the spatial sequence. The fact that likelihood and necessity have such wide application, together with the fact that they cannot account for the complete unity of tragedy, is also proof that this structural criterion is not the ultimate principle of tragedy. For the ultimate principle must be that which establishes tragedy's total nature as an existing thing.

V. *Plot as Quantitative Organization, Chapter 12*

Chapter 12 deals with a completely different sense in which plot is an organization of tragedy. For besides being organized as a form or structural unity through the likelihood and necessity of its incidents, tragedy is also organized in a quantitative or material sense in that the on-going succession of incidents is divided into discrete sections which the Greeks called episodes but which we today call acts or scenes. These discrete sections are parts of tragedy in a completely different sense than are the formal parts discussed in chapter 6. For acts, scenes, and episodes have a temporal duration, and one ceases when another begins. But the six formal parts are all parts of tragedy as a whole, for it is ridiculous to suppose that at a given point in a drama there is, for example, the end to a section devoted to plot and the beginning of a section containing diction or character. The formal parts can be imagined, if you will, as a vertical hierarchy of forms encompassing the entire drama. The quantitative parts will then be divisions in time along the horizontal sequence of incidents.

The problem in this chapter is how these divisions are to be effected. The answer is that each quantitative part is to be a whole. That is, each part will have a beginning, middle, and completion, not in the sense of completing the likelihood and necessity of a sequence of incidents, but in the sense of constituting a temporally separable phase of that total sequence. A convenient word to use in order to signify such a phase in the complete action of a drama is the Greek word "agon," which means simply contest or struggle. For the most part the term has been applied to the quantitative divisions of Greek comedy, but it is a term eminently suited to refer as well to what Aristotle conceived to be the principle of the quantitative divisions of tragedy. The on-going flow of incidents is thus to be divided into units having the completeness of an agon which is to be known by its separability within the sequence. For acts and scenes cannot with effect be started or completed at any chance point. Since even choral odes are subject to the same principle, the term agon may be extended to include them also, for they must also constitute wholes.

Changes in the conventions of theater since the days of Greek drama should not lead one to suppose that the problem discussed in this chapter is peculiar to the tragedy of those days simply because the quantitative parts of which Aristotle speaks are those found in Greek tragedy. Analyses of the changing styles in the theater may discover important distinctions between the quantitative divisions of Greek tragedy with its regular alternation of episodes and choral parts and the innovations introduced by later periods. But Aristotle's problem is one that cuts across such stylistic differences and is as germane to twentieth-century drama as to that of his own day. In fact, among many contemporary writers the quantitative organization of art would seem to be regarded as even more important than the formal organization which Aristotle thought was the prior consideration of the two. For example, in discussions of instrumental music the essentials of musical organization are usually found by distinguishing such forms as sonata allegro, theme and variation, rondo, etc. But these are not "formal" organizations in Aristotle's sense of the term, but rather different kinds of quantitative organization. For each of these is defined according to the fashion in which it divides up the temporal sequence of the sound.

VI. *Plot as Functional Organization, Chapters 13-16*

Chapters 13-16 are concerned with the examination of a third sense in which plot is the organization of tragedy. This is the sense in which plot achieves an affective function or proper pleasure. The principle of this functional organization in the case of tragedy is the catharsis of pity and fear. There has probably been as much discussion and debate over this principle as there has been over any other part of Aristotle's philosophy. It has been given interpretations of almost every conceivable kind, but mainly ethical, rhetorical, or psychological. The interpretation to be given here is the one which is already implicit in the approach to art which we have been slowly explicating.

We have already hinted at the fact that catharsis has several senses all derivative of the fullest catharsis found in a complex plot having reversal or recognition. Chapters 13-16 attempt to outline the problems connected with this complete sense of the term. The derivative senses of catharsis, we will find, are all due to the peculiarities of the poet's argument, i.e. the poetical idea which he seeks to express. The derivative senses will therefore be discussed when we come to chapters 17 and 18 where Aristotle examines the process by which this argument is realized. In this section of the analysis we will be concerned only with catharsis in its most complete form.

The affective function of plot has four factors which constitute the four causes of tragedy's proper pleasure. Catharsis, we will find, is the principle which accounts for all four. The affective meaning or proper function of a tragic plot in its most complete form consists in the fact that a reversal of fortune (discussed in chapter 13), arising through a tragic mistake (discussed in chapter 14), befalls a character (discussed in chapter 15), and issues in a recognition (discussed in chapter 16). The four chapters thus discuss, in order, the (1) *what,* (2) *how,* (3) *to whom,* and (4) *why* which give the plot its tragic meaning. That is, they are the four causes (respectively, the formal, efficient, material, and final) of the final cause or function of plot. For the character is the material upon whom the form of reversal is imposed, the mistake is the moving cause which gives that form to the material, and the recognition is the end or function attained.

Aristotle opens chapter 13 with the explicit statement that it is the end aimed at or the function of tragedy which is now to be discussed. He further states that this function is to be examined as it is achieved in the most beautiful form of tragedy, the complex plot, and then lays down the criterion for that discussion, the attainment of tragedy's proper affections, pity and fear.

Four kinds of reversal, in a problematic order, are then examined. Since it was previously determined that tragedy imitates what is better rather than what is worse, and since what pity and fear would seem to have in common is their concern with misfortune, the first kind of reversal considered is that of a man preeminently good changing from good to bad fortune. This is rejected because it is repulsive and not piteous and fearsome, for what is piteous and fearsome cannot repudiate our sense of human worth. A correction is sought by changing both the character of the agent and the direction of the reversal, but this solution to the problem is rejected on the same grounds. For good fortune is as unworthy of the wicked as misfortune is of the best of men. At this point we have not attained a structure of events that is even humane, much less piteous and fearsome. The only alternative now is to vary the two factors of the reversal (the character and the direction) independently. Since changing the character would give us good men changing to good fortune and this is obviously neither piteous nor fearsome, the third alternative must change the direction of the reversal. This at least produces the humane rather than the repulsive, but a final change is still necessary to produce the piteous and fearsome. This is accomplished by changing the character, not to what is better in the fullest sense (for this would repeat the mistake of the first form considered), but to the mean or one like us. But since average virtue entails acts both good and bad, and since if it is evil intentions which bring misfortune on the doer the pity of the misfortune is negated, it is necessary that the reversal be due to a mistake or a "missing of the mark."

This argument, as far as its general features are concerned, is a good illustration of Aristotle's problematic method. For it shows clearly how the several factors or causes of a situation are weighed and tested in their in-

terrelations to attain a solution, i.e. a statement setting
forth their unity in accordance with a principle. In particular the argument indicates the dependence of two
factors (the character of the protagonist and the source
of the reversal) on the affective requirements of that
reversal. For it is in order that the reversal be piteous
and fearsome that the other two are given their characteristics. The discussion of the mistake and of the character in chapters 14 and 15 must therefore be condi-
tioned by this consideration. Finally, the argument also
exhibits what appears to be an affective requirement of
all art—namely, that if each species of art is to have its
appropriate pleasure, the very possibility of art starts
with the necessity that the affective function be humane,
i.e. befitting or appropriate to human values and not
repulsive.* The humane would then seem to be an affective function common to all art, including comedy
which, within the sphere of the humane, is the contrary
of tragedy.

It is in the context of this argument determining the
tragic reversal that the affections of pity and fear are
defined. Perhaps the most important thing to notice is
that they are not defined by reference to audience re-
actions, nor are they defined even as emotions or passions of the soul. They are instead defined as objective
qualities of the dramatic incidents. An emotion in the
psychological sense, as we learn from Aristotle's general
theory of motion, is a passion or a "being moved" by
something else, and in all motion it is the form of the
agent that arises in the patient. If, therefore, the audience is to feel pity, that pity must already be the form
of the object which moves the audience. However harsh
it may sound to our ears, it follows that pity is in the
tragedy itself as a form, and there is no reason in Aristotle's approach to art to seek the signs of pity in the

* This is also implied in Aristotle's discussion of censures
in chapter 25. See p. 141.

suffering of the audience. It will be noticed that at times
Aristotle uses the expression "the piteous" rather than
"pity." If pity is the quality of an incident, the piteous
will be the incident itself insofar as it has that quality.

As an objective quality of the incidents of a tragedy
pity is said to be "concerned with misfortunes that are
undeserved." For an incident to be undeserved it must
depend for its meaning on preceding incidents, for a
misfortune cannot appear as undeserved unless the previous actions of the character make it so. Pity, therefore,
is the tragic meaning which present incidents have in
relation to the past. Necessity, we have seen, is also a
relation between present and past. But necessity is the
possibility or believability of the past in relation to the
present, while pity is an affective property of the present
in relation to the past. Aristotle says that "fear is concerned with misfortunes that are similar," but he does
not say to what they are similar. In general, fear is an
anticipation of impending misfortune, and unless what
is expected finds its potentiality in present events there
is no fear. As a quality of dramatic incidents, therefore,
fear must be the similarity of future misfortune to the
potentiality of present incidents. Fear, therefore, is related to likelihood as pity is to necessity. For as pity is
the meaning or function which a tragic incident has in
its relation to past incidents, so fear is the meaning
which a tragic incident has in its relation to what is future. Fear is therefore the tragic meaning which likelihood imparts to the present as pity is the tragic meaning
which a necessity imparts to the present. Plot, therefore,
has reflexivity in its affective meaning analogous to the
reflexivity in its structure, for it is the incidents of the
plot which give themselves their tragic meaning.

In chapter 13, as we have seen, the requirements of
the tragic reversal make it necessary, in the complex
plot, for the misfortune to be accomplished through a
mistaken action rather than through wickedness or evil

intention. Otherwise it would not be piteous and fear-some as an act but only as a suffering. The process by which the reversal comes about is examined in chapter 14. In the first paragraph it is stated that the piteous and the fearsome misfortune should arise from the construction of the incidents and should produce, not the monstrous, but the piteous and the fearsome. Since the pleasure arising from pity and fear (i.e. their catharsis) is brought about by imitation (a synthesizing of form and matter), "this pleasure must be produced in the incidents."

The characters on whom the agent brings misfortune must be those he loves, else there is no pity or fear in his act but only in their suffering, and as chapter 6 established, tragedy is primarily concerned with action. It is important, with respect to an understanding of the nature of recognition as well as with respect to the proper interpretation of a disputed point in the discussion of character in chapter 15, that the criterion here given, the love of characters for one another, be kept in mind. For in respect of the criterion of pity and fear it is not necessary that tragic characters be good, but only that they love what they harm, and as Aristotle says in the next paragraph, what the agent recognizes is that love.

The structure or form of the process by which the misfortune is brought about has four possibilities, for the action can either be done or not done, and either knowingly or in ignorance. For suffering or misfortune to be brought about knowingly would mean that it could not be the action that is piteous or fearsome, but only the suffering itself. In such plays, therefore, the tragic protagonist would have to be the one who suffers, not the one who acts. And if the tragic misfortune is not even accomplished, then the play lacks even the pity and fear of suffering. It is therefore the worst of all constructions for tragedy. But since tragedy is essentially an imitation of action, the better forms of tragedy will find their pity and fear in action. Consequently, the complex plot having either reversal or recognition, and not suffering alone, will bring about the misfortune by a mistaken action of the protagonist, an action done in ignorance, and essentially ignorance of the fact that the misfortune has fallen on one he loves. Again, there are two possibilities, for the mistake can either be done or not and therefore the misfortune can either be brought about or not. Of the two Aristotle says the best is the one in which the misfortune does not occur because the protagonist recognizes his mistake in time and therefore does not do it. Several reasons for his choice can be found. First of all, a misfortune which is only imminent or impending and does not actually occur is just as piteous and fearsome, while impending, as one that eventually does occur. The only way in which it could fail to be piteous and fearsome is if it were established that it could not happen. But obviously, at that point it would no longer be imminent. Secondly, to have the misfortune or suffering actualized introduces pain and therefore the possibility of the monstrous, and the monstrous is inimicable to the tragic pleasure. But the most important reason is that it is when the misfortune is not actualized, being prevented by a recognition, that the principle and proper pleasure of tragedy, the catharsis of pity and fear, is most complete. We must turn, therefore, to the explication of this principle.

The essential features of catharsis are already implicit in our discussion of chapters 13 and 14. Catharsis in general is a purgation or elimination of one thing from another of which the first was a part, this constituting a cleansing of the former from the latter. In the definition of tragedy in chapter 6 Aristotle states that tragedy achieves "through pity and fear a catharsis of such affections." It is therefore pity and fear themselves which achieve their own catharsis from tragedy. This means that in the function of tragedy what is active and what is passive are the same, for pity and fear are said to act upon themselves. This fact constitutes the ultimate reflexivity of catharsis, and this reflexivity we should be able to discover implied in the discussions of the tragic reversal and hamartia above. For if pity and fear are formal properties of the incidents of tragedy, so is their self-caused elimination.

That which is common to pity and fear is their concern with misfortune. The explication of their catharsis should therefore start from this notion of misfortune in order to establish the connection they have to one another within the affective organization of tragedy. Let us start with the catharsis of pity. Any misfortune which the protagonist brings upon either himself or those he loves (and a misfortune to a loved one is essentially a misfortune to oneself) must consist in a worsening of the mode of living which he has hitherto enjoyed. It must involve the loss of something of great value in that life, such as his economic or social position, the things or people he especially loves, or, at the extreme, his own life. If the misfortune or loss actually occurs the only way in which the pity of the loss can be eliminated in a way consistent with the importance placed upon the loss, is by making that very loss the means by which an even greater value is realized. For if pity is undeserved misfortune, and if in the fulfillment of that misfortune the protagonist shows by the manner in which he faces his loss a courage and nobility which outweigh the thing he has lost, then in terms of those higher meanings developed by the plot, his fortune has been a gain and not a loss, and instead of undeserved it is in a more significant sense deserved. For it is without meaning to pity a man who has lost a lesser good in gaining a greater. The catharsis of pity, therefore, is a function of the reversal. Moreover, it is pity that catharts pity. For the quality of the protagonist's action which makes the misfortune unpiteous is the very quality which made it piteous in the first place.

Fear is the similarity of impending misfortune to the potentialities of the present. Unlike pity, which is the affective meaning of present incidents as they are related to the past, fear is the affective meaning of present incidents as they are related to the future. Pity was catharted when the affective meaning of past incidents transformed the meaning of present incidents to make them no longer undeserved. By analogy, fear must be catharted when the affective meaning of future incidents transforms the meaning of present incidents to make them no longer similar. Now the past can effect present action directly without the mediation of thought, and therefore the proper vehicle for the catharsis of pity is the reversal. But the future can effect present action only indirectly through the mediation of thought, and therefore the proper vehicle for the catharsis of fear is recognition. For recognition is a change of thought, as reversal is a change of action. The catharsis of fear consists in the recognition by the protagonist of those values which are essential to his character and actions, but of which he has lost sight when contemplating the mistake which produces his misfortune. This shows us why the vehicle by which fear is catharted is called recognition, ἀναγνώρισις, and not merely discovery, εὕρημα. For the protagonist re-cognizes, ἀνα-γνωρίζω, what is already of value to him. He does not discover, εὑρίσκω, any values unrelated to his past. For this would only produce the catharsis of fear at the expense, not only of the catharsis of pity, but of pity itself, since if he had not had those values previously the misfortune would not have been undeserved. The catharsis of fear, then, is accomplished when a future misfortune ceases to have a similarity to present potentialities. Since those present potentialities for the misfortune must be found in the present actions of the protagonist as they exhibit his intentions which are a function of his state of knowledge, it is only by changing that state from ignorance to knowledge that the similarity of the impending misfortune can be negated. The catharsis of fear is thus a function of recognition. Moreover, it is fear itself which catharts fear. For the very similarity of the impending misfortune to the present potentialities of the protagonist's actions, as recognized by the protagonist, makes the impending misfortune no longer similar.

Our discussion of the nature of catharsis started with the problem why Aristotle decided that the best tragedy is the one in which recognition prevents the occurrence of the reversal. It should be noted that in order to discuss the catharsis of pity we used the example of the second best form of plot, the one in which reversal is actualized, while in order to discuss the catharsis of fear we used the best form of plot, the one in which recognition precludes reversal. To decide why the latter is better than the former we shall examine what happens to fear when the reversal occurs and then what happens to pity when recognition prevents reversal.

When the recognition occurs either during the performance of the mistake or after the reversal has been accomplished, it merely sustains the catharsis of pity which the reversal provides, for it helps to make more evident the higher values which the reversal is designed to exhibit. This is because the recognition must consist in the explicit statement of precisely those values. But the similarity of the potentialities of the previous incidents to the impending misfortune (which constitutes fear) is literally fulfilled since the misfortune actually occurs, and therefore in a literal sense there is no catharsis of fear. The recognition makes the previous incidents dissimilar to what actually ensues only in the sense that the values which the protagonist exhibited in the mistake are rejected in the recognition for the higher values which the reversal led him to recognize. But this is no more than what was meant by saying that the recognition only supports the catharsis of pity when the reversal occurs. The catharsis of fear through recognition in a plot constructed about a reversal is thus quite like the effect of a "recognition" (in a derivative and inferior sense) in a plot of suffering. For in a simple plot in which the pity and fear are occasioned by a force acting *upon* the protagonist, there can be a "recognition" in the sense that the protagonist can recognize the values which are being destroyed by that force. But in this sense the "recognition" does not produce catharsis and the plot is not complex.

On the other hand, the catharsis of pity fares better when reversal is precluded by recognition than does the catharsis of fear when the reversal is actualized. For though the deservedness of the protagonist's fortune does not rise out of its undeservedness (for the undeserved misfortune does not occur), still what does arise is literally *not* the undeserved, and therefore to this extent there is a catharsis of pity. Furthermore, the values exhibited in the tragic recognition are precisely those which would have catharted the pity of the impending misfortune had it occurred. There is a sense, therefore, in which both catharses can be effected in this kind of plot, and to this extent it is better.

The catharsis of pity and fear in the fullest sense as found in a complex plot thus establishes the completion of the affective function of tragedy. That is, the catharsis of pity and fear is the highest form of tragedy's proper pleasure. For pity and fear are most pleasant, not simply as affections, but when they are resolved or completed, and affections are motions which can be completed only by ceasing to be. A simple plot can establish the proper affections, but it cannot satisfy the mood it creates. In a complex plot there is, in the very incidents of the tragedy, a release of the tensions which constitute its affective function. A simple plot does not relieve these tensions, and therefore it is less pleasant.

What is more, the catharsis of pity and fear determines the completion, not only of the affective organization of a tragedy, but its structural organization as well. The mere fact that a tragedy, any tragedy, is constructed of incidents shows that it involves change. But the change in the sequence of incidents in a simple plot is indefinite. The change in a complex plot, on the other hand, has a beginning and an end which mark the *terminus a quo* and the *terminus ad quem* of a unity in the fullest sense, for they are the marks of a completed change. It is in this sense that the best constructed play, one with a complex plot, is an imitation of one action. For the one action is the change which the protagonist produces, in his own action, through reversal or recognition. All the incidents in the tragedy are simply the specification and explication of the circumstances and conditions from which the change arises and into which it is completed.

Having discussed those problems relating to the reversal and the hamartia, Aristotle turns in chapter 15 to problems concerning the dramatic characters. The chapter divides into four parts, each concerned with a different aspect of the construction of characters. The first paragraph discusses four criteria to which characters should conform when regarded in themselves apart from their function in the all-embracing synthesis of the plot. That is, they are four ways in which the poet's rendering of characters can be successful, regardless of whether or not he is successful in his organization of the sequence of the incidents. They are therefore four senses in which characters can be characters in the fullest sense.

The most important thing concerning the full delineation of characters is that they be of that sort which makes what they do appear to be precisely what is implied by their characters. But what establishes character in the first place is the human values revealed in action. This is why Aristotle repeats his statement that there will be character only if there is choice, for it is what a character chooses, as indicated by either words or deeds, that shows what sort of person he is. A character is effective* if his actions are seen to follow from what he is, but this can be the case only if the choices that establish that character are in turn effective in exactly the same sense. The effectiveness of a character therefore consists in a reflexivity whereby the choices which constitute a character must be such as to account for the choices he makes in the drama. A character is therefore effective or dramatically successful in the highest sense when it is itself the source of such choices as constitute its nature. As Aristotle says, any kind of character can be made effective in this sense, even if the character be inferior or base—that is, even if the values exhibited in the choices are in themselves imperfect. It is on the basis of this criterion of effectiveness that Aristotle criticizes Euripides' characterization of Menelaos in the *Orestes*. For the villainy which Menelaos exhibits in his speech

---

* Most translators have translated χρηστόν in this passage as "good" rather than "effective." They have done so with the assumption that Aristotle was laying down a moral criterion for tragic characters. But this interpretation is not only inconsistent with what poets have historically found to be tragic, but also contrary to the spirit of Aristotle's own statements concerning character. For he says the tragic character should not be equitable or good, but like the average (1453ᵃ 7), and he may even be worse in some respects (1456ᵃ 21). What is most important for the purposes of tragedy is not *what* he values, but the fact that he *destroys* what he values (1453ᵇ 19). It is this that makes even morally bad characters like Medea piteous and fearsome. If χρηστόν is to be translated as good it must be with the understanding that morally bad characters can also be "good" in the dramatic sense intended by Aristotle.

to Orestes is not necessary in order to make the character a convincing source of his actions.

The second mark to aim at in the establishment of characters is their suitability. A character is suitable if his traits are all appropriate to the type of character which that character himself establishes. It might be perfectly suitable for a female character to be represented as clever, but not if she is also represented as womanly.

Thirdly, in addition to being the clear source of his own actions and the fulfillment of his own type, a character should be similar to or like the probabilities which the dramatic situation develops. For what kind of characters are apt to appear in situations depend upon the nature of those situations, and characters are badly constructed if they do not reflect the probabilities of the circumstances in which they are found.

Finally, the character should be consistent in the sense of exhibiting a continuity throughout the sequence of incidents. That is, he should keep to the sort of character he is represented as being, even if he is represented as being the "sort" of character who does not fall under any particular "sort." All four of these criteria of character, as we have said, can be met whether or not the poet achieves a unity in his sequence of incidents. This point will be important when we come to examine chapter 18, for it is this fact which makes possible the plot of character which Aristotle mentions there.

In the three remaining paragraphs of chapter 15 Aristotle considers the construction of characters as this relates to other aspects of the drama. In the second paragraph of the chapter he considers the relation of characters to the plot construction. In this relation characters as well as incidents are brought under the principle of likelihood and necessity. For likelihood and necessity are structural relations among incidents in their sequence and will therefore govern characters, not as characters, but only as they account for relations between incidents. The major problem here is the avoidance of the contrivance—that is, the introduction of an unlikely character whose function is to unravel the complications developed in the plot. Since a contrivance makes the sequence episodic it is better relegated to incidents narrated by characters rather than those depicted on stage. In the third paragraph Aristotle examines the relation of character to the thoughts which characters express. The character of a man includes the way in which he stands in respect to the emotions—his tendencies in respect to anger, for example. The emotions, as Aristotle says in the *Rhetoric,* are the things which alter the judgments of men. This effect of character on thought finds its extremes in irascibility and its contrary, inirascibility or evenness of temper, since anger is the emotion which most affects the thoughts we express. On the other hand, it is the equitable man whose judgments are most fair and in accordance with reason. Therefore, since tragedy imitates the better rather than the worse, it is appropriate that the emotional weaknesses of the characters be counterbalanced by making the character otherwise equitable or of fair judgment. In the fourth and last paragraph of the chapter Aristotle makes a passing reference to the relation between character and spectacle, for the visible aspect of characters may add or detract from the characterization intended.

Chapter 16 is concerned with the end or function which the affective organization of plot attains, the recognition in which a sequence or a part of a sequence issues. The primary problem in effecting a recognition therefore lies in its relation to preceding incidents. For the recognition is the primary means of producing the astounding, but as we have seen, the astounding is more astounding when unexpected or unlikely incidents prove to have arisen with likelihood. The five forms of recognition are thus five ways in which recognitions rise out of preceding incidents with varying degrees of likelihood. They range from the almost episodic connection through signs and heirlooms to the strongest connection in which the recognition rises from the reversal itself, whether this be imminent or actualized.

VII. *Plot as Effected Organization, Chapters 17-18*

Chapters 13-16 were concerned with the affective organization of tragedy. That is, they were concerned with the way in which the plot is organized in the attainment of tragedy's proper pleasure, the catharsis of pity and fear. As we have indicated, the properties of tragedy which were explicated in those chapters were those which tragedy attains only in its most complete form, the complex plot. For it is in the complex plot that the complete sense of catharsis is realized. But not all tragedies are complex in their organization, for not all tragedies achieve the full catharsis of pity and fear which the nature of tragedy makes possible. The cause of this fact is to be found in the nature of the poetic argument, the germinal idea from which the poet begins in his construction of a tragedy. For the extent to which the proper pleasure of tragedy is effected in the tragedy depends upon certain peculiarities of the tragic conception which the poet is trying to realize. The very nature of the argument which the poet conceives as containing the essence of the tragic may preclude the full achievement of catharsis. This is a matter quite independent of the question of whether or not the poet has successfully articulated his tragic idea. That is, the cause of incomplete catharsis here considered is not simply the poet's lack of art, his failure to achieve likelihood and necessity in his construction. Rather, as we will see, different kinds of poetic argument result in different kinds of likelihood and necessity as well as different kinds of catharsis.

The fourth sense in which plot is the organization of tragedy is thus to be traced to the process in which the poet proceeds from a tragic idea in germinal form to its complete realization as a concrete work of art. For the nature of this process through which the poet goes and the factors involved in this process, especially the poetic argument itself, will condition the organization which the tragedy attains. To the examination of this process by which the organization of tragedy is attained Aristotle devotes chapter 17 and 18. These chapters thus constitute an inquiry into the efficient cause of the plot or organization of tragedy, as chapters 7-11 dealt with its formal cause, chapter 12 with its material cause, and chapters 13-16 with its final cause.

Chapters 17 and 18 divide the problem of the process of constructing tragedy into its two essential phases of potentiality and actuality. For chapter 17 deals with the four conditions from which this process arises, while chapter 18 deals with four aspects of the concrete fulfillment of this process as this appears in the work of art. This division is thus quite comparable to the way in which the problem of the genesis of the species was divided in chapters 1-5. The first paragraph of chapter 17 examines the problem of the visual appearance of the incidents and the need for visualizing them in order to avoid incongruities. The second paragraph examines the problem of making the incidents functionally effective and the need for the poet's empathy. The last two paragraphs consider the poet's argument which contains the germ of the final construction and the episodes which constitute the material expansion or the "filling out" of the argument. From the point of view of the process through which a tragedy is generated the plot is thus the argument plus the episodes.

The discussion of the argument is especially important with a view to understanding Aristotle's meaning of plot. The argument or poetic idea from which the poet starts his construction is the skeleton of the action, the barest essentials of the change represented in the drama. One and the same argument can be used by different authors in different tragedies which establish completely different likelihoods and necessities. For this reason Aristotle calls the argument universal. Plot, on the other hand, is the particular realization of this universal, the concrete interconnection of all that occurs in the drama. It is the actual synthesis of the incidents in which character, thought, diction, melody, and spectacle are all actualized. The argument is only the potential synthesis. Plot is therefore the drama in its most concrete sense, and it is impossible for two tragedies to have the same plot and still be two tragedies. The argument is the abstract, the synopsis of the drama. The distinction is important to keep in mind since in contemporary writings the term plot is usually employed in the sense which Aristotle gave to the term argument.

In illustrating his notion of argument with the example of *Iphigenia in Tauris* Aristotle distinguishes between incidents external to the plot and incidents external to the argument. The distinction is possible only because the universal argument extends more widely than the plot. The plot contains whatever is acted or occurs on the stage. If an event occurring off stage or before the action of the play is narrated by a messenger on the stage, then the narration of the event is a part of the plot, but not the event itself. The event itself, however, is still part of the argument. Whatever is neither acted nor narrated is external to both plot and universal argument. This distinction will be important when we come to chapter 24, for having unreasonable incidents within the universal argument, but external to the plot, is not as objectionable as having them within the action of the plot.

Chapter 18 turns to the effects of this process of construction on the organization of tragedy. In the first paragraph the sequence of the drama is distinguished formally into two parts, the involvement and the solu-

tion. In a complex plot achieving catharsis the involvement is that part of the sequence which establishes the
dramatic tension of pity and fear. The solution is then
that part of the sequence which establishes the release of
that tension. Involvement and solution are therefore
the formal phases of the sequence corresponding to the
affective phases of tension and release. They are easiest
to distinguish in a complex plot, and therefore it is a
complex plot which Aristotle uses as an example. But
as the first sentence says, every tragedy has these two
phases to its sequence, even though the sense in which
a tragedy has them may be quite derivative. What this
means can be seen as we discuss the implications of Aristotle's next paragraph.

The four forms of tragedy listed in this next paragraph are four kinds of organization which the nature
of tragedy permits the poet. They are the various levels
at which the function of tragedy can be achieved. That is,
they constitute a hierarchy of kinds of tragedy ranging
from the complex plot which relates incidents to their
greatest possible unity down to that form which achieves
the least unity consistent with the tragic function. They
are therefore four ways in which tragedy achieves the involvement of a dramatic problem and reaches a solution.
Which of these forms is used by the poet in a particular
construction depends on the nature of the germinal idea
or argument from which he starts the process of construction. But what forms are available as realizations of
poetic arguments depends on the nature of tragedy. For
the four forms are all parts of tragedy's dramatic function as this was outlined in chapters 13 and 14. That is,
the pity and fear which constitutes tragedy's proper pleasure was seen in those chapters to depend upon the
actions of characters (their reversals and recognitions),
their effects upon one another (their sufferings), what
sort of persons they are (their characters), or the visual

presentation of the incidents (spectacle*). As Aristotle says in this paragraph, the best tragedies make each of these parts contribute to the dramatic function. But since the poet's argument may preclude this, tragedies can be said to be more or less tragic according to which of these sources of pity and fear and how many of them are utilized in the drama. The four forms of tragedy (the complex plot, the plot of suffering, the plot of character, and the plot of spectacle) result from the choice of the poet of one of these four parts as the ultimate source of the dramatic function and unity. This choice is implicit in the tragic argument which he seeks to realize. The four forms thus represent the latitude within which the nature of tragedy gives the poet freedom in the determination of his organization while still achieving, to some degree, tragedy's proper pleasure.

The complex tragedy is, as we have seen, the imitation of an action. For the change in the sequence of incidents is brought to a completion by making either an actual or imminent misfortune of a character the consequence of that character's own action. But what happens can be represented as action only if the dramatic situation gives the characters latitudes of choice. Such latitudes of choice can be represented in the drama only if the likelihoods of previous incidents are *not* continuously realized as the sequence is unfolded. The very essence of action in the dramatic sense is the unexpected. But as we saw in the analysis of chapter 9, the unexpected is most effectively realized if, though previously unlikely, it exhibits its likelihood when it arises. The likelihood of the unlikely is thus essential to the depiction of action. For nothing that arises without the sense of novelty or initiation can be viewed as action.

But the imitation of an action not only necessitates

* The determination of tragedy's proper pleasure through spectacle is referred to at 1453^b 1.

the likelihood of the unlikely. It requires as well that what eventuates be related to the purposes of the agent. That is, the incidents should not only be unexpected, but also wondrous rather than simply astounding. For, as we have seen, the wondrous is the realization, with likelihood, of an unlikely incident which is related to the choice or moral purpose of the characters involved. The astounding is the realization, with likelihood, of an unlikely incident which is not related to the intentions of characters. The astounding is thus simply the unexpected realization of the forces operating in a dramatic situation. It is attained simply by showing the sequence of incidents to be the unlikely consequences of the way in which characters affect one another. Where the unexpected is merely astounding, therefore, the most that can be achieved is the imitation of suffering, not action. For the unexpected can reveal action only if it can be connected to a character's plan or purpose.

These considerations will enable us to see the logic behind the list of four forms of tragedy given by Aristotle. For each form of tragedy is the result of an abstraction from the power of tragedy which is realized in the preceding and higher form. When the plot is so organized as to be the unfolding of unexpected but believable incidents which derive their meaning from the intentions of characters, the poet has achieved a complex plot of action which issues in reversal or recognition and the relations between the incidents are wondrous. The first abstraction consists in removing the intentions of the characters. The plot then becomes the unfolding of unexpected but believable incidents which are meaningful only as the effects of characters upon one another. The poet has then achieved a simple plot of suffering in which reversal and recognition are precluded and the relations between the incidents are only astounding since intention is not involved. The second abstraction consists in removing the unexpected completely. The plot then becomes the unfolding of the previously established probabilities determined by the propensities or habits of the characters who make up the dramatic situation. The poet has then achieved a simple plot of character in which nothing unlikely occurs. The third abstraction consists in removing the characters as sources of the likelihood of incidents. The plot then becomes the unfolding of probabilities which incidents have simply as incidents. The characters in the drama are not used to account for what happens, but simply represent types who conform to the probabilities already inherent in the incidents. The poet has then achieved a simple plot of spectacle since the likelihood of the sequence is a function of the visual presentation of what happens.

These four kinds of plot will achieve four related senses of catharsis and four related senses of likelihood and necessity. In other words, they will exhibit four kinds of poetic pleasure and four kinds of unity, the lower forms derived from and therefore inferior to the higher in the sense that the less complete organizations will only partially fulfill the power which defines tragedy. But though tragedies can be distinguished as better or worse in this general way on the basis of the principle of catharsis, it does not follow that all tragedies should be complex. For what is proper to a complex tragedy would be episodic if used to realize an argument which, by its nature, requires the structure of a plot of character. Such a mistake is, in fact, exactly what Aristotle meant by a contrivance. Each poet is therefore to be estimated in terms of the "good" in which he excels— that is, in terms of the form of plot which is implied by the nature of the tragic conception from which he works. A just estimation of a poet's work thus views the solution of a plot, not in terms of what tragedy in general is able to achieve, but in terms of the tragic conception articulated in the involvement or complication. For the four kinds of argument produce four kinds of involvement, and each kind of involvement requires its proper kind of solution or denouement, the other three kinds being episodic to it.

In general, the turning point or climax of the plot which separates involvement and solution will occur when the sequence has fulfilled the likelihoods which relate the incidents to one another. In a complex plot, as we have indicated, this fulfillment is not brought about until the tragic action is completed, for it is not until then that the likelihood of the sequence as a whole is apparent. So also in a plot of suffering the likelihoods of the sequence would be established only after the sequence had exhibited the consequences of the parallelogram of forces constituting the dramatic situation. In both of these higher forms of plot, then, the turning point of the drama would tend to come near the end of the sequence. In a plot of character, however, the likelihoods of the sequence are established as soon as the characters constituting the dramatic situation have been so delineated as to account for what follows. So also in a plot of spectacle the involvement ends as soon as the incidents have established their likely consequences. In these two lower forms of plot, therefore, the turning point tends to be earlier. But the poet can, of course, employ devices designed to delay the turning point in order to heighten the effect. The four kinds of turning points differ from one another not so much by virtue of when they occur, but by virtue of what it is they complete, for as we have seen they complete four kinds of likelihoods. Because they are the completions of different kinds of relations between incidents these four kinds of turning points have different degrees of dramatic effectiveness and give greater or less clarity to the distinction between involvement and solution. In a complex plot the turning point is most climactic, for it is not only unexpected, but it is also the point at which the dramatic tension is relieved. On the other hand, the turning point in a plot of spectacle is difficult to place and affords no relief at all.

All of the terms used in the examination of the function of tragedy in chapters 13-16 have three forms of incompleteness or degradation resulting from the three abstractions from the complete sense of catharsis. The pattern of this degradation can be seen if we trace one of these terms, the tragic mistake or hamartia, through the four forms of plot. In a complex plot the hamartia is essentially an action, a missing of the mark in the sense that a character has himself brought harm to the very things he values. In a plot of suffering the hamartia is not an action but a passion, a state to which a character is brought by opposing forces in the dramatic situation. In a plot of character the hamartia is a flaw of character, the general tendencies constituting a man's nature which account for the incidents of which he is the cause. In a plot of spectacle the hamartia is a tendency implicit in the nature of the incidents rather than in the nature of the characters, since the characters appear simply as stereotypes which symbolize the effectiveness of the course of events in producing misfortune. Pity and fear can be brought about by any of these four senses of hamartia, but it is clear that the most piteous and the most fearsome is the hamartia of action. For it can include all that is piteous and fearsome in the others and in addition the notion of self-infliction which gives the misfortune its highest intensity.

VIII. *The Diction of Tragedy, Chapters 19-22*

As chapters 7-18 were concerned with the ultimate organization of tragedy when tragedy is considered as a self-subsistent entity, chapters 19-22 are concerned with the ultimate material of tragedy under the same consideration. This material is diction. But diction is not

the antecedent material on which the poet places the
form of human action, for that material is speech. Poetic
diction is rather that formal part of tragedy, organized
or constructed by the poet himself, which serves as the
ultimate material for the higher forms of organization,
thought, character, and plot. For the diction that the
poet uses in tragedy is an artifact having a poetic purpose and is not to be confused with other forms of diction used in other disciplines for other purposes. This
accounts for the marked differences between Aristotle's
discussions of language in the *Poetics,* the *Rhetoric,* and
his works on logic. The four chapters on diction will
therefore be concerned with the four causes constituting
the nature of language constructed for poetic purposes.
The four chapters deal with the efficient, material, formal, and final causes of that construction in that
order.

Character was considered in chapter 15 as the material
cause of plot's affective organization, and its relations to
plot and to thought were discussed there. Of the two
intermediate organizations between plot and diction,
therefore, only thought has not been examined. In the
first paragraph of chapter 19 Aristotle mentions this
fact, but says that thought presents no problems to poetic
science that are not covered adequately in the *Rhetoric.*
He therefore proceeds in that paragraph merely to list
the four forms (*ἰδέαι*) which exist in tragedy by virtue of
thought, for these forms constitute the four ways in
which diction is organized to constitute thought. That
is, these are the four kinds of things which characters
can effect through the articulation of their diction into
thoughts. The four forms of thought guide the discussion of diction insofar as the function of diction is to
achieve a structure from which these four forms are able
to arise. When characters speak they are either, 1. demonstrating (i.e. showing that in the dramatic situation

certain things follow from the assumption of other things), 2. solving (i.e. finding the cause by which opposing factors constituting a problem in the dramatic situation can be interrelated so that action can proceed), 3. rendering the passions (i.e. effecting another character's passions through speech), or 4. maximizing and minimizing things (i.e. altering the apparent importance of factors in the dramatic situation). These forms, Aristotle says, can also emerge from the incidents or the happenings on stage as well as from what the characters say. For incidents also can effect the piteous, the fearsome, the maximal (i.e. exaggeration), or the likely. The two lists differ insofar as incidents cannot constitute demonstrations or solutions to problems. The analogue to these two as far as incidents are concerned is the likely. But the function of speech, Aristotle cautions, is not to make the meaning of incidents apparent, just as the function of incidents is not to make the meanings of speeches apparent. For if either the incident or the speech is in itself without meaning it has no place in the plot. Words and deeds each have their proper function, and a drama is not successful if either is used to make up for the shortcomings of the other.

The second paragraph begins the discussion of diction by first distinguishing that aspect of diction which is irrelevant to poetic science, its declamation or delivery. For words change their meanings by virtue of the manner in which they are spoken, so that a prayer can be made to sound like a command, a factual description like a threat, and an innocent question like a dogmatic conclusion. But the art of giving words their proper intonation and emphasis so as to produce the correct meaning is one that belongs to the performer, not to the poet. For it is precisely what the poet writes that is subject to varieties of oral interpretation. For this reason problems concerning the way in which diction arises in performance can be set aside as irrelevant to poetic science.

In chapter 20 Aristotle discusses the material cause from which poetic diction is to be constructed. This material ranges from the element of voice (of which the written sign is the letter of the alphabet), through successively higher linguistic organizations, to speech which is the highest synthesis of voice. Aristotle goes through his list of eight parts showing how each of them functions as a material for the next form, and then shows in his examination of the highest synthesis, speech, what it is that grounds the whole sequence.

The vocal elements are elements—that is, the ultimate result of analysis—in the sense that when they are divided their parts are the same in kind or form as the elements themselves. That is, they are homogeneous in structure, for a part of the sound "a" is still the same sound. Vocal elements are the materials out of which syllables are synthesized. Neither elements nor syllables are in themselves significant, nor do they have any function in the determination of significance. Conjunctions and joints are syntheses of syllables and vocal elements which achieve a higher form of organization. For while conjunctions and joints do not themselves have significance, they do have a function in relating parts of speech that are significant. Joints effect higher organizations of speech than do conjunctions. For articles and pronouns, which are examples of joints, make more specific, and therefore more significant, relations among parts of speech than do prepositions and particles (such as "and," "but," and "while"), which are all conjunctions in Aristotle's sense of the term. That is to say, "and" does not produce a synthesis, but merely indicates that two things are simultaneously considered. A conjunction like "on" or "before" establishes a relation between two things, but the two things remain two things. Articles and pronouns, however, which are joints, show that two sections of speech signify the same thing, and therefore establish the highest synthesis of all those parts of speech which are not in themselves significant.

Nouns, verbs, cases, and speeches all differ from the other four part of diction in having in themselves significance—that is, a literal denotation of existing things. For "therefore," "since," "after," and such parts of speech are unmeaning in themselves just because they do not denote things. They are what are called *syncategorematic* words. But "apple," "ran," "John's," and "two times four" all refer to or denote existents in successively higher complexes of existence. They are what are called *categorematic* words. A noun or name has bare significance. A verb both signifies something (as "ran" signifies a kind of motion) and also indicates time. It is therefore not on the same level of synthesis as a noun, for it synthesizes additional things which a noun cannot synthesize. When nouns and verbs are considered, not as such, but in respect of their case, it is obvious that the case synthesizes, not only everything synthesized in the noun or verb, but also the relation which constitutes the proper function of the case.

Finally, speech synthesizes everything synthesized by the lower syntheses into the highest of all organizations. Speech itself has two kinds of synthesis or unity. For if one were to say "John went to the store. While he was there he met Jim," the speech would lack strict unity because what is designated is not one thing, but a conjunction of things set in certain relations. This is the kind of unity which any work of literary art attains, for a work of literature is always about a conjunction of things in their interrelations. As we have repeatedly said, the unity of a work of art is not derived from its literal copying or signification of an existent thing. Instead the work develops an internal principle of unity which still does not give it a necessary nature in the sense in which an oak tree has a necessary nature. On the other hand, a scientific treatise on a subject matter—for example, even the *Poetics* itself as a treatise on a tragedy—has a unity in a far more significant sense. For however various the words, phrases, sentences, paragraphs, and chapters, they are all ultimately predications of a single object and have the same unity that the object attains to the extent that they reproduce that unity. Since, however, the subject matter of natural science has stricter unity than the subject matter of poetic science (for the nature of a natural object has necessity while the nature of tragedy is not necessary), a treatise on physics has even greater unity than the *Poetics*. The ultimate criterion, therefore, for all linguistic organization is the organization afforded by the significance of speech and the significance of speech lies in the unity of the object denoted or signified. All lesser parts of speech find their function within the governance of this ultimate function.

Chapter 21 is concerned with the formal cause of poetic diction—that is, the peculiar or proper structure of such diction. The form of speech generally, as we have seen from chapter 20, is the form of the object it signifies or represents. What poetic diction does is to structure the way in which speech signifies its object. For in poetry words do not relate to their objects in the direct fashion which was found in chapter 20 to constitute the significance of common speech. Instead poetic diction relates the word or vehicle of diction to its object obliquely or indirectly in order to gain eloquence and poetic beauty. These oblique relations have the effect of putting the word vehicle at a further distance, so to speak, from its denoted object. The way in which the word is related to its object as a result of this removal constitutes the form of poetic diction.

Incidentally, it should be pointed out that the Greek

word (ὄνομα) translated as "word" in this chapter and the next is the same word translated as "noun" in chapter 20. Yet in his illustrations of forms of diction Aristotle uses verbs and cases as well as nouns. He uses the term "noun" because it is insofar as the higher parts of speech perform the same kind of function as nouns that they can be given poetic forms. We have translated "noun" as "word" in order not to impair his meaning by violating contemporary idiom.

The discussion of the form of poetic diction has three parts. In the first paragraph words are distinguished according to the number of parts they contain which are significant, not within the word, but by themselves in separation from the word. The important point is that no matter how many significant parts the word has, the word is significant only as a whole and not by virtue of the conjunction of those significant parts. For within the word "Theodore," as Aristotle says in chapter 20, the "dore" no longer means gift.

In the next three paragraphs are discussed the eight forms of diction by which the relationship of meaning between a word and its object is structured for poetic purposes. They are arranged in order according to the degree to which the word is separated from the object to which it refers. The foreign word produces the greatest possible separation, while in the authoritative or customary word there is no poetic separation at all. In chapter 22 Aristotle calls "strange" all those words in which a poetic structure is given to the word's significance. A foreign word is thus the "strangest" of all poetic forms. An authoritative word is one that is not strange at all. The metaphor stands next to the foreign word, and there are four kinds of metaphors listed in the order of their strangeness. When a genus is used instead of a species the meaning is more obscured than when a species is used instead of a genus. The meaning is even less obscure if the metaphor replaces a species with another species within the same genus. Finally, when the metaphor is based on an analogy the four terms involved in the analogy give a direction to the meaning intended. This is especially true if the word related to the word implied is also given. For example, the meaning is more obscure if one refers to the bow of a ship as "the nose" than if one refers to it as "the nose of the ship." In Aristotle's list of strange words the ornamental comes next after the metaphorical, but it is the only one that he does not bother to define. The ornamental would appear to be a word which, though significant in itself, does not add any significance which is not already present in the speech, but is rather included to fulfill the requirements of the meter. Such a word would be produced if another related word were added to the analogy just given. For in saying "the jutting nose of the ship" the word "jutting" adds nothing not implied by the other words, yet it might be necessary to the meter. By a made-up word Aristotle does not mean one coined *de novo,* for this would constitute a foreign word and as strange a word as one could get. A made-up word, as he indicates, is rather one that is derived from a different part of speech. One might, for example, call someone a "sedentarian" because he inclined to laziness. In this case the noun would have been derived from the adjective. Extended words and contracted words are even closer to authoritative words. Closest of all, however, is the altered word which is like the made-up or derived word, but only in respect of a part, not the whole word. For example, if "conformitation" were used instead of "conformity." For here it is only the suffix that is derived, not the noun itself.

The last paragraph in the chapter discusses the relation between the significance of words and the vocal elements in which they terminate. For while the ancient

Greeks did not employ rhymed endings in their verses as we do, they understood the importance of a fitting use of assonance and consonance within the meter. In chapter 20 attention was drawn to the vocal element as such. In chapter 21 where the question is how poetry structures significance, it is only in respect of the genders of words that a relationship can be established between what the word means and what sounds it contains, and genders determine only end-sounds.

In chapter 22 the proper function or final cause of poetic diction is determined. In the first paragraph this function is said to be the attainment of significance without the triteness which typifies vernacular speech. Authoritative or customary words have the greatest significance, but produce triteness. Foreign words and metaphors produce the greatest dignity of expression, but by themselves produce barbarisms or enigmas. The first paragraph thus lays down the end of poetic diction and the material potentialities from which that end can arise. Paragraph two turns to the way in which this end can be attained, i.e. by blending the words so as to attain something between these two unwanted extremes. It finds that those strange words least removed from authoritative words are especially efficient in this respect. Yet they will not produce either the beauty of foreign words and metaphors or the clarity of authoritative words. The third paragraph discusses the criterion of moderation which such blendings are to achieve, for an unfitting use of the poetic forms of diction will fail to achieve their purpose. In the last paragraph the various forms of diction are related to various species of art whose proper functions will determine which of these forms are most suitable to those functions. It is in this paragraph that the ultimate dependence of diction on the requirements of plot is most evident.

IX. *Tragedy as the Expression of a Poetic Argument, Chapters 23-26*

Chapters 23-26 are concerned with the last of the three main divisions of the *Poetics*. In the first division, chapters 1-5, tragedy was examined as efficient cause. For in the interest of determining the nature of tragedy through an examination of the process by which it arose as a species, the ultimate cause of that nature was found to be that nature itself as it slowly articulated itself by determining its own specific properties. In the second main division, chapters 6-22, it was not tragedy as a cause of genesis that was investigated, but tragedy as a composite whole, a form or organization imposed on material parts, independent of the conditions from which it arose. In the third division, chapters 23-26, tragedy is examined as an end or final cause. What this means can best be stated by contrasting the discussion in these chapters with the discussion in chapters 7-18.

In the latter chapters, when the problem was the determination of tragedy's formal cause or organization, the discussion proceeded from the definition of tragedy which fixed the framework of the discussion, through the various requirements which that definition entailed, till finally in chapters 17 and 18 it could be determined what the latitudes were within which the poet could work while still producing a work of art more or less conforming to the definition. What this latitude provided for was the variability in the argument or germinal idea from which the poet begins his construction. In a literal sense, therefore, one could say that those chapters examined the place of the poet's argument within the bounds of the definition of tragedy. In chapters 23-26 it is the opposite problem which is discussed. For here what is examined is the place of various species of art within the requirements of the poet's argument. That is, in chapters

7-18 the problem was to determine what is involved in the construction of a given species of art and how the function of that species may be used as the criterion of the various factors that are involved in that construction. Among those factors were the alternative poetic ideas of the tragic. Here the problem is rather to determine what is involved in the realization of a poetic idea and how that idea can be used as the criterion of the various factors that are involved in its realization or expression. Among those factors are the alternative species of art which are able to fulfill the poetic argument. It is therefore precisely what was fixed in the former discussion— namely, the defined species—that is variable in the latter. It is precisely what was variable in the former discussion—namely, the poetic argument—that is fixed in the latter, for it is the argument that defines the problem in the last four chapters. Chapters 23-26 therefore treat tragedy as a final cause, for it is not here considered simply as an organization of parts, but as an end in artistic expression.

A poetic argument which is the germ of a work of art must already contain in itself, but incipiently, the poetic function which the concrete work will realize. For otherwise there can be no basis for any comparison of poetic species as its possible realization. The only species of art which in Aristotle's day could be compared with tragedy as the fulfillment of an argument was epic. For only epic shared with tragedy the catharsis of pity and fear. It is, in fact, the need for such a comparison that explains why so much space is devoted to epic, for the characteristics of tragedy have been adequately covered. In these four chapters, therefore, it will be the catharsis of pity and fear in its germinal form that will be the criterion in the investigation of the four causes involved in the expression of an argument. Thus, for all the diversity in the problems of the three main divisions of the *Poetics,* the principle governing the solutions to those problems is in each case the same.

In the expression of a poetic argument one of the factors to be considered is the structural organization which is most appropriate to the argument. This is the subject of chapter 23. In the first paragraph it is the general difference in structure between tragedy and epic that is considered. The argument itself will indicate whether it can best be realized within the stricter unity of tragedy or the more loosely constructed epic form which consists in the imitation of a multiplicity of actions. In order to develop the characteristics of epic it is compared with both tragedy and history. Epic differs from tragedy because, though it imitates an action that is as unified as it can be, its action is diversified by events related to but outside of that action. Epic differs from history because history finds its unity in a single time span and not in a unity of action. Arguments which are proper to epic should therefore be those which need an organization intermediate to the extremes of history and tragedy.

Besides implying a general organization of the sort just considered, the argument will also imply an organization in a more specific sense, and the second paragraph of chapter 23 turns to consider this more specific organization. As we have indicated in our discussion of chapter 18, the argument will determine whether the plot will be complex, of suffering, of character, or of spectacle. That is, the argument will determine which of the four parts by which incidents are meaningfully related will be the ultimate organization of the work. If this is so, then, in deciding whether one should construct a tragedy or an epic, it is important to see if either species has any limitation in this respect. But Aristotle states that the four parts are shared by the two species.*

---

* Epic, of course, does not have spectacle, and therefore it would be inappropriate to call the fourth form of epic a plot

The specific organization implied by the argument will also make it necessary to ask whether epic and tragedy have the same formal parts listed in chapter 6. Epic lacks two of these; melody and spectacle. If therefore the argument demands these as means of heightening the function, tragedy will be a more suitable form of expression.

It is worth noting that when Aristotle classifies the *Iliad* and the *Odyssey* he does so by giving each of them a double classification. For he says that the *Iliad* is *both* simple and of suffering, while the *Odyssey* is *both* complex and of character. But we have seen in the case of tragedy that a plot of suffering is itself simple and therefore the description of the *Iliad* seems redundant, while a plot of character is *not* complex and therefore the description of the *Odyssey* seems contradictory. But if we consider the difference between epic and tragedy an explanation can be found. For tragedy imitates a single action, or ought to. But epic by its very nature is the imitation of an action which, though unified, is amplified and extended by the use of incidents related to but not part of the main action. Epic, therefore, has by its nature two problems where tragedy has only one. For the main line of incidents in epic can itself be any one of the four kinds of organization given in chapter 18, depending upon what it is that gives likelihood and necessity to this central core of the work. But the extensions and amplification which are related to but not part of this central core must also be related by some form of likelihood and necessity. That they cannot be related as incidents are related in a complex plot is clear from their very definition. It therefore follows that there will be two statements to be made concerning the organization of an epic: one stating the organization of the main core of the plot; another stating the relation between

of spectacle. But it would still be an organization in which the likelihood of the sequence arose simply from the incidents themselves, in this case narrated rather than performed.

this core and the amplifying incidents which give it magnitude. This will explain why the *Odyssey* can be both complex and of character.*

The problem of chapter 24 concerns, not the total organization implied by the argument (whether general or specific), but the way in which the argument can be articulated sequentially or from a quantitative point of view. This chapter thus deals with the material aspect of the problem of expression, dividing itself into four parts indicated by the four paragraphs. The first paragraph compares epic and tragedy as magnitudes. That is, it regards the sequential needs of the argument in terms of the total length. Here the larger magnitude of epic is aided by its narrative manner, since this allows the simultaneous presentation of many incidents which find appropriateness to the magnificence which is proper to the epic magnitude. The second paragraph compares the materials out of which the sequence is built in the two species of art and finds an appropriateness in the heroic meter to the massiveness of epic, as chapter 4 found iambic appropriate to the conversational and dramatic diction of tragedy. The third paragraph concerns the role of the maker in this sequence—that is, the amount of that sequence which the poet can assign to himself by injecting his own thoughts into the poem. In the case of tragedy this intrusion of the poet is discussed by implication in the last paragraph of chapter 18. In discussing this subject here Aristotle is not referring to the fact that in epic the incidents are narrated throughout by the poet. He is speaking of irrelevant intrusions upon the narrative—as when in a preface the poet in-

---

* It is because Aristotle is anticipating his later statements about the *Iliad* and the *Odyssey* that he sets up the distinctions between simple and complex, of suffering and of character, in the first sentence of this paragraph, instead of listing the four forms he discussed in chapter 18, i.e. plots that are complex, of suffering, of character, and of spectacle.

vokes the Muse in his own person, or when at any time
he departs from the plot to express his own generaliza-
tions. The last paragraph deals with the affective function of the sequence. The epic, because of its narrative
and the ornateness of its diction, is more easily able to
use the unreasonable and therefore better able to achieve
the wondrous or the likelihood of the unlikely.

Chapters 23 and 24 were concerned with the problems
of finding an artistic organization or species of art which
would give definition to a poetic idea or argument, either
as a structural whole (chapter 23) or as a quantitative sequence of parts (chapter 24). Chapter 25, on the other
hand, is concerned with problems which arise in the
realization of a poetic idea which *cannot* be solved by
reference to the requirements of a species of art in which
the argument may be realized. These problems, therefore, concern aspects of the poet's construction within
which a species of art allows the poet the freedom to
make his own decisions without prejudice to the achievement of the function of that species. These problems can
therefore be solved only by reference to the intentions
of the poet in that area within which the species gives
him latitude. As the organization of the chapter shows,
the problems are located at the two poles involved in his
construction: the form of his imitation (i.e. the object
he chooses to imitate) and the matter of his imitation
(i.e. the language in which he chooses to imitate). Chapter 25 thus examines the problems involved in the
expression of a poetic idea as they relate to the efficient
cause of that expression, as chapters 23 and 24 examined
respectively those problems related to the formal and
material causes of that expression.

The first paragraph of chapter 25 first lays down the
two areas in which such problems are to be found, i.e.
(1) what the poet imitates and (2) the words in which he
chooses to imitate. In respect of the first the poet has

the freedom of choosing one of three kinds of objects: either the true, the seeming, or the better. In respect of the second the poet has the freedom of choosing either authoritative words or strange words. The paragraph goes on to distinguish first (1) between rightness in poetic science and rightness in other areas such as politics, and then, within poetic science itself, (2) between mistakes which are essential to poetic science and mistakes which are accidental to poetic science. For what Aristotle has to guard against is the supposition that the problems he is going to deal with can be solved either (1) by bringing in irrelevant ethical, psychological, rhetorical, or other criteria, or (2) by reference to the requirements of the species constructed. We shall see that all of these problems are to be solved strictly by going to the intentions of the artist, since these intentions constitute the solutions to the censures of his choices.

The next paragraph lists the six defenses which the poet has at his disposal against censures relating to what he has imitated. They are the solutions to problems relating to the choices he is free to make within the species of art he is constructing, and his ability to defend himself against such censures should guide him in making those choices. The six justifications of his choice of what is imitated are: 1. Though the poet produced a mistake, such as the imitation of something that is impossible in nature, it was necessary to achieve the function of the species of art. 2. The mistake is one according to some other discipline, not according to the requirements of the art involved in this construction. 3. What is imitated is what ought to be. 4. What is imitated is what seems to be—that is, what men suppose or opine. 5. What is imitated is what is the case—that is, what is true. 6. What is imitated is morally justified by the situation in which it takes place. As Aristotle says in the last paragraph of this chapter, these six solutions are all answers to five

kinds of objections or censures to which all censures can
be reduced—namely, that what is imitated is either 1.
impossible (i.e. cannot happen in fact), 2. unreasonable
(i.e. is not probable in fact), 3. noxious (i.e. offensive to
moral sensibility), 4. incongruous (i.e. inconsistent or
contradictory in relation to something else in the drama),
and 5. against rightness according with some art (i.e.
against the procedures or findings of some other discipline). As Aristotle says in the fifth paragraph of this
chapter (the next to the last), the solutions vary in their
ability to justify the object imitated depending upon the
censure which can be brought against the object. For
example, it would seem that if a poet is censured because something that happened in his drama was lewd,
the best defense would be the sixth if it could be made,
and while the first and the fifth might be effective defenses, the third would be ridiculous to the extent that
there was any justice to the censure.

The third paragraph of the chapter lists those solutions to the same five censures which relate, not to the
object which the poet has chosen to imitate, but to the
words in which he has chosen to imitate. Again, there
are six defenses at the poet's disposal. They are that 1.
the word chosen is a foreign word and therefore has a
different meaning than the one assumed in the censure,
2. the word is to be taken metaphorically, not literally,
3. the word is meant to be pronounced differently and
this will change its meaning, 4. the syntactical structure
of the expression has been misunderstood and this mis-
understanding has altered the word's meaning, 5. the
word has another authoritative meaning besides the one
assumed, and 6. the word has been used in accordance
with its customary meaning, not the one assumed. These
six defenses against censures relating to the words
chosen, plus the six defenses against censures relating
to the object imitated, which were discussed above, are

the twelve solutions to which Aristotle refers in the clos-
ing sentence of the chapter.

The understanding of chapter 25 is crucial to the grasp
of Aristotle's general approach to art, for it explains a
great deal by implication concerning the meaning of his
conception of art as an imitation of nature. In section I
of this analysis when the general nature of imitation was
being considered, the object imitated was said to be a
perceptible form which had an existence prior to the
poet's construction. In section II, when chapter 2 was
being examined, it was found that the objects imitated
are primarily distinguishable, for poetic purposes, according to their affective significance. As affective or
emotional significances these forms were distinguishable
into two kinds, the morally superior and the morally inferior, for this distinction was found to be the one which
controlled the proper pleasure of the work of art. The
function of the poet, therefore, is not to construct pity
and fear themselves, for these are the conditions of art
which the artist finds as qualities existing prior to his
construction. His function is rather to construct an
artificial thing which has pity and fear as its formal
qualities. But lest the reader suppose that this antecedent
form served as the organizing principle of the work of
art determining its unity and poetic value, it was quickly
added that there is within the art work itself a criterion
which serves that purpose. To the explication of that
internal principle most of sections III to VII were devoted, with the conclusion that while pity and fear are
the antecedent objects of imitation, their catharsis is
the proper function of the work of art and something
not found in nature prior to art, but achieved by the
poet in his construction.

What chapter 25 does is to allow us a fuller grasp of
the sense in which pity and fear, or any other perceptible
forms, are antecedent conditions of art. For when Aris-

totle distinguishes between that which is, that which is
said to be, and that which ought to be, and when he
says that the poet may choose between any of these as
the thing he imitates, he makes it clear that not only is
the function of art independent of extrinsic considerations found in other disciplines, but even the antecedent form utilized by the poet is independent of those
other considerations. For as long as a work of art is regarded as an existing thing having a definable nature
in and of itself (i.e. as long as the problems of art are
considered as problems of producing that nature), and
as long as that nature leaves certain matters indeter-
minate because the decision on these matters does not
affect the success or failure of the production of that
nature, then any choice in these matters, however essential it may be to some other discipline such as science
or morals, must remain gratuitous to art. Neither the
truths of science nor the prudential considerations of
ethics, therefore, can dictate, for the solution of productive problems, whether the poet should imitate the
true, the seeming, or the better.

Yet this does not mean, even from a productive view-
point, that the poet is thereby free to violate truth or
offend moral sensibility. Chapter 25 is concerned with
establishing solutions to problems posed by censures of
what the poet has chosen, but this implies that unless a
poetic justification can be given the censure is just. The
poet therefore is not free to choose the impossible, the
unreasonable, the morally noxious, the incongruous, or
what contradicts the standards of rightness in any art as
he is free to choose between the true, the seeming, or the
better. For he must find a defense against any of the five
censures, but the three possible objects of imitation
themselves constitute possible defenses. The reason why
solutions are needed to these five censures is not stated
by Aristotle, but it should be evident from his whole

approach to art. For the function of an art is its proper
pleasure, and mistakes of any sort must detract from that
pleasure unless they are specifically needed to attain it.
Both the censures and the solutions to them, therefore,
to the extent that both are justified, find their justification, as far as tragedy and epic are concerned, in the
catharsis of pity and fear.

The final chapter of the *Poetics* is concerned with the
function to be attained by the expression of an argument or poetic idea in concrete form. For the problem
of finding a suitable species in which to realize a poetic
argument must also take into consideration the question
of which of the possible species best fulfills the function
implicit in that argument. After answering the objections
against tragedy's superiority, Aristotle lists in the third
paragraph four considerations which serve to establish
the conclusion that the pleasure common to tragedy
and epic is better fulfilled in tragedy. 1. In respect of
the pleasures that derive from the various formal parts,
none of those involved in epic are lacking in tragedy
since it possesses all the parts which epic has. In fact,
tragedy has the advantage of two parts, melody and
spectacle, which are not in epic. The pleasures of these
parts cannot be dismissed, even though they are not the
principal pleasures of tragedy. 2. What is concentrated
is more pleasurable than what must go on at greater
length, so that in respect of its quantity or magnitude
also, tragedy is poetically superior. 3. Tragedy is also
superior in being a better vehicle for the poet in his
attempt to bring his work of art together to a unity.
For when epics are used to satisfy this desire the result is
inimical to the very nature of the epic. 4. Finally, the
most important consideration is that tragedy is better
able to achieve the function which it has in common with
epic: the catharsis of pity and fear. This follows from
the fact that epic cannot achieve the integration of

tragedy. The four considerations are thus respectively the formal, material, efficient, and final causes of the end at which the expression of a poetic argument aims.

INDICES

INDEX OF PROPER NAMES

INDEX OF TERMS

With the exceptions to be noted below, this index aims
to be an exhaustive reference to every term used by Aristotle
in the *Poetics*. If there is an occurrence of an English word
in the translation without a reference in the index it is
because the Greek text merely implies that word. Where
more than one Greek term has been translated by the same
English word the Greek terms are listed separately under
the English word. Where more than one English word has
been used for the same Greek term the variants are enclosed
in parentheses after the Greek term. It should also be noted
that, due to the peculiarities of both Greek and English,
words appearing in the index as nouns, for example, may
in the translation appear as other grammatical parts.

The only Greek expressions omitted from the index are
particles, connectives, prepositions, pronouns, and the like,
a few common adjectives and adverbs, and a few common
verbs such as εἰμί (to be or exist), ἔχω (to have or possess),
γίγνομαι (to become or arise), χράομαι (to use), δέω (ought
to), ἐρῶ and εἶπον (to express or mention), λέγω (to speak),
and φημί (to say). The only term of importance omitted is
τραγῳδία (tragedy), since, being the subject of the *Poetics*,
it appears throughout. Those words quoted by Aristotle
from other authors are also omitted.

abject, ταπεινός—1458ᵃ 18, 20,
32

able, δυνατός (possible)—1455ᵃ
29

able, to be, δύναμαι (possible,
to be)—1450ᵃ 36, ᵇ 5

about, to be, μέλλω—1447ᵃ 10,
1453ᵇ 18, 21, 34, 38, 1454ᵃ 6,
8, 1455ᵇ 9, 1459ᵃ 33

abroad, to be, ἀποδημέω—
1455ᵇ 17

absurd, ἄτοπος—1460ᵃ 1, 35,
ᵇ2, 1461ᵇ 5

accidental, συμβεβηκός—1460ᵇ
16, 30

accusation, κατηγορία, ἡ—
1462ᵃ 5

accuse falsely, to, συκοφαντέω
—1456ᵃ 5

accustomed, to be, ἔθω—1447ᵇ
17

goddess, θεά, ἡ—1455ᵇ 5

good, ἀγαθός—1450ᵃ 28, 1451ᵇ 37, 1454ᵇ 9, 1456ᵃ 6, 1459ᵇ 29, 1460ᵇ 2, 1461ᵃ 8

go through, to, διέξειμι—1449ᵃ 31

grasp, to, λαμβάνω (gain, to, seize, to; take on, to)— 1453ᵇ 15

grave, βαρύτης, ἡ—1456ᵇ 33

grievous, οἰκτρός—1453ᵇ 14

grow, to, αὐξάνω (increase, to) —1449ᵃ 13

guard, φύλαξ, ὁ—1461ᵃ 11

habituation, συνήθεια, ἡ— 1447ᵃ 20

hamlet, κώμη, ἡ—1448ᵃ 36, 38

handed down, παρειλημμένος —1453ᵇ 22

happen (by chance), to, συμβαίνω—1448ᵇ 9, 16, 1451ᵃ 13, 17, 25, ᵇ8, 29, 1452ᵃ 19, 28, 35, ᵇ3, 1453ᵃ 7, 21, ᵇ6, 1454ᵃ 13, ᵇ1, 1455ᵃ 8, ᵇ6, 1458ᵃ 12, 1459ᵃ 23, 1460ᵃ 13

happen (by fortune), to, τυγχάνω—1447ᵃ 15, 25, ᵇ9, 1450ᵃ 3, ᵇ32, 33, 36, 1451ᵇ 13, 1452ᵃ 35, 1453ᵃ 18, 1459ᵃ 24, 1460ᵇ 24, 36, 1462ᵇ 13, 15

happen (by fortune) to meet, to, ἐντυγχάνω—1461ᵇ 5

happiness, εὐδαιμονία, ἡ— 1450ᵃ 17

happy, to be, εὐδαιμονέω— 1450ᵃ 20

harmony, ἀρμονία, ἡ—1447ᵃ 22, 23, 26, 1448ᵇ 20, 1449ᵃ 28, ᵇ29

hear, to, ἀκούω—1453ᵇ 5, 6, 1455ᵃ 2, 1459ᵇ 30

hearing, ἀκρόασις, ἡ—1459ᵇ 22

heroic, ἡρωικός—1448ᵇ 33, 1459ᵃ 10, 11, ᵇ32, 34

hexameter, ἑξάμετρος—1449ᵃ 27, ᵇ21

hinder, to, κωλύω (prevent, to) —1461ᵃ 34

historian, ἱστορικός, ὁ—1451ᵇ 1

history, ἱστορία, ἡ—1451ᵇ 3, 6, 7, 1459ᵃ 21

hit upon, to, στοχάζομαι (aim at, to)—1456ᵃ 20

honored, ἔντιμος—1449ᵃ 6

horn, κέρας, τό—1457ᵇ 35, 1460ᵇ 31

horse, ἵππος, ὁ—1460ᵇ 18

house, οἶκος, ὁ—1455ᵇ 19

household, οἰκία, ἡ—1453ᵃ 19, 1454ᵃ 12

humane, φιλάνθρωπος—1452ᵇ 38, 1453ᵃ 2, 1456ᵃ 21

hymn, ὕμνος, ὁ—1448ᵇ 27

iambic, ἰαμβεῖον, τό—1448ᵇ 31, 1449ᵃ 21, 25, 26, 1458ᵇ 19, 1459ᵃ 10, 12, ᵇ37

idiomatic, ἰδιωτικός—1458ᵃ 21, 32, ᵇ1, 4, 1459ᵃ 3

ignorance, ἄγνοια, ἡ—1452ᵃ 30, 1453ᵇ 35, 1456ᵇ 13

ignorant, to be, ἀγνοέω (know, to not)—1453ᵇ 30, 1454ᵃ 2, 1459ᵃ 4, 1460ᵃ 6

imitate, to, μιμέομαι—1447ᵃ 17, 19, 26, 28, 1448ᵃ 1, 8, 16, 18, 20, 21, 24, 26, 28, 29, ᵇ5, 20, 25, 1450ᵃ 10, 11, 20, ᵇ29, 1454ᵇ 9, 11, 1459ᵃ 12, ᵇ25, 1460ᵃ 9, ᵇ9, 17, 29, 31, 1462ᵃ 10

imitation, μίμημα, τό—1448ᵇ 9, 18

μίμησις, ἡ—1447ᵃ 16, 22, ᵇ13, 15, 21, 29, 1448ᵃ 7, 24, ᵇ3, 8, 35, 1449ᵃ 32, ᵇ10, 24, 31, 34, 36, 1450ᵃ 4, 16, ᵇ3, 24, 1451ᵃ 31, ᵇ28, 1452ᵃ 2, 13, ᵇ1, 33, 1453ᵇ 12, 1454ᵃ 27, ᵇ8, 1459ᵃ 15, ᵇ33, 37, 1461ᵇ 26, 1462ᵇ 1, 4, 5, 11

Gateway Titles

GENTZ, FRIEDRICH, & POSSONY, *Three Revolutions*

HANNA, THOMAS, *The Thought and Art of Albert Camus*

HARVEY, WILLIAM, *On the Motion of the Heart and Blood*

HEIDEGGER, MARTIN, *Existence and Being*

HITTI, PHILIP K., *The Arabs—A Short History*

HOBBES, THOMAS, *Leviathan I*

HOFFMAN, FREDERICK J., *Modern Novel in America*

HUME, DAVID, *Enquiry Concerning Human Understanding; Abstract of A Treatise on Human Nature*

JASPERS, KARL, *Nietzsche and Christianity*

JOHNSON, HOWARD A. AND NIELS THULSTRUP, *A Kierkegaard Critique*

JOHNSON, SAMUEL, *Lives of the English Poets*

JUENGER, F. G., *The Failure of Technology*

KIRK, RUSSELL, *The Conservative Mind*

KLAASEN, ADRIAN, *The Invisible Hand*

LEONHARD, WOLFGANG, *Child of the Revolution*

LEWIS, WYNDHAM, *Self Condemned*

LOCKE, JOHN, *Essay Concerning Human Understanding* (Abridged)

LOCKE, JOHN, *Of Civil Government*

LOCKE, JOHN, *On the Reasonableness of Christianity*

MACHIAVELLI, NICCOLO, *The Prince*

MAISTRE, JOSEPH de, *On God and Society*

MARCEL, GABRIEL, *Man Against Mass Society*

MARCEL, GABRIEL, *Metaphysical Journal*

MARCEL, GABRIEL, *The Mystery of Being,* Vols. I & II

MARCUS AURELIUS, *Meditations* (with EPICTETUS, *Enchiridion*)

MARX, KARL, *Das Kapital* (Abridged)

MARX, KARL, *Communist Manifesto*

MAYER, PETER, ed., *The Pacifist Conscience*

MILL, JOHN STUART, *Considerations on Representative Government*

MILL, JOHN STUART, *On Liberty*

MORLEY, FELIX, *Freedom and Federalism*

NIETZSCHE, FRIEDRICH, *Beyond Good and Evil*

NIETZSCHE, FRIEDRICH, *Philosophy in the Tragic Age of the Greeks*

NIETZSCHE, FRIEDRICH, *Schopenhauer as Educator*

NIETZSCHE, FRIEDRICH, *Thus Spoke Zarathustra*

O'CONNOR, WILLIAM VAN, *An Age of Criticism*

PICARD, MAX, *Man and Language*

PICARD, MAX, *The World of Silence*

PICO della MIRANDOLA, GIOVANNI, *Oration on the Dignity of Man*

PLATO, *Euthyphro, Crito, Apology, Symposium*

RICOEUR, PAUL, *Fallible Man*

ROUSSEAU, JEAN JACQUES, *The Social Contract*

RUEFF, JACQUES, *The Age of Inflation*

SARTRE, JEAN PAUL, *Existential Psychoanalysis*

SENESI, MAURO, *Longshadow and Nine Stories*

SMITH, ADAM, *The Wealth of Nations* (Selections)

SOROKIN, PITIRIM A., *Fads and Foibles in Modern Sociology*

SOROKIN, PITIRIM A., *The Ways and Power of Love* (first 15 chapters)

SOSEKI, NATSUME, *Kokoro*

SPENGLER, OSWALD, *Aphorisms*

SPENGLER, OSWALD, *Selected Essays*

STEVENSON, ROBT. LOUIS, *Selected Essays*

SUMNER, WM. GRAHAM, *The Conquest of the United States by Spain and Other Essays*

THURSTON, HERBERT, *Ghosts and Poltergeists*

TILGHER, ADRIANO, *Homo Faber: Work Through the Ages*

UNAMUNO, MIGUEL de, *Able Sanchez & Other Stories*

VIVAS, ELISEO, *Creation and Discovery*

VIVAS, ELISEO, *The Moral Life and the Ethical Life*

WEAVER, RICHARD M., *The Ethics of Rhetoric*

WRIGHT, DAVID MCCORD, *Capitalism*